COOKING WITH HEIRLOOMS

Seasonal Recipes with
Heritage–Variety Vegetables and Fruits

COOKING WITH HEIRLOOMS

Seasonal Recipes with Heritage–Variety Vegetables and Fruits

By Karen Keb Acevedo
with recipes compiled and tested by Carol Boker

HOBBY
H F
FARM
PRESS

An Imprint of BowTie Press®
A Division of BowTie, Inc.
3 Burroughs
Irvine, California 92618

Karla Austin, *Business Operations Manager*
Nick Clemente, *Special Consultant*
Barbara Kimmel, *Managing Editor*
Jessica Knott, *Production Supervisor*
Deibra McQuiston, *Design Concept*
Amy Stirnkorb, *Designer*
Indexed by Melody Englund

Amanda Boyce: 18, 21. Erik Boker and food stylist Laura Hathaway: 6, 16, 22, 31, 36, 40, 49, 57, 78, 84, 87, 88, 101, 109, 121, 122, 133, 138, 143, 144, 151, 152, 155, 161, 162, 167, 173, 176, 186, 193, 207, 208, 221. Dennis Burchard Photography: 156, 182, 183, 185. David Cavagnaro: Cover, 2, 10, 26, 28, 29, 33, 38, 48, 51, 52, 54, 55, 76, 92, 103, 106, 108, 116, 118, 135, 136, 139, 148, 153, 160, 164, 177, 187, 191, 209, 219, 225. Sharon P. Fibelkorn: 93, 123, 168, 170, 213. Autumn Foushee: 39. Sandy Hevener: 90, 174. Larry Javorsky: 25. Karen Keb Acevedo: 27, 44, 62, 67, 74, 81, 83, 94, 96, 98, 102, 111, 112, 115, 125, 145, 158, 170, 171, 179, 189, 204, 214, 217, 218. Diane Lackie: 91, 140, 147, 194. David Liebman: 104, 100, 110. Al Michaud: 86. Fran Jurga: 128, 131. Jennifer Nice: 70, 71, 73. Robert Ott: 46. Photos.com: 6, 8, 11, 19, 24, 32, 35, 36, 42, 45, 47, 50, 53, 56, 58, 59, 60, 61, 64, 66, 68, 88, 89, 97, 105, 112, 113, 119, 124, 126, 129, 142, 149, 150, 166, 169, 178, 180, 190, 192, 199, 201, 202, 205, 206, 210, 211, 215, 216, 220. Kirk Schlea: 165. Shutterstock.com: 89, 199, 202. Bonnie Sue: 19, 30, 134. Esther Thompson: 63. Adria Weatherbee: 203.

Library of Congress Cataloging-in-Publication Data

Acevedo, Karen Keb.
  Cooking with heirlooms : seasonal recipes with heritage–variety vegetables and fruits / by Karen Keb Acevedo with recipes compiled and tested by Carol Boker
      p. cm.
  Includes bibliographical references and index.
  ISBN 978-1-933958-01-9
  1. Cookery (Vegetables) 2. Cookery (Fruit) 3. Vegetables—Heirloom varieties. 4. Fruit—Heirloom varieties. I. Boker, Carol. II. Title.
  TX801.A24 2007
  641.6'51—dc22
                          2007002837

BowTie Press®
A Division of BowTie, Inc.
3 Burroughs
Irvine, California 92618

Printed and bound in Singapore

16 15 14 13 12 11 10 09 08 07   1 2 3 4 5 6 7 8 9 10

DEDICATION

For my wise friend Michelle Iten, who has nurtured and inspired my interests in gardening, cooking, personal history, and spirituality. Thank you for keeping me grounded.

ACKNOWLEDGMENTS

RECIPE CONTRIBUTORS

Carrie Whealy, Seed Savers Exchange
Amanda Boyce, Shady Elm Farm
Lisa Leber, Filaree Farm
Bill and Dayna Yockey, Townline Farm Poultry Reserve
Sandi Weller, Prairie River Farm
Liz Zorn, Peace Angel Farm
Kristin Mehus-Roe
Michelle Iten
Maggie Oster
Arlene Coco
Joel Girardin
Margaret Haapoja
Mildred Trump
Victoria Storm
Chef Kevin Fielding
Chef Andrea T. Morris
Laura Hathaway
Carol Boker
Karen Keb Acevedo

RECIPE TESTERS

Victoria Storm
Chef Andrea T. Morris
Frances Stephens
Thomas and Rachel Barthel

CONTENTS

FOR THE LOVE OF HEIRLOOMS

I am not an expert on heirlooms, nor have I been saving seeds for many years. I am someone who is captivated by history, particularly American history, in all of its forms, who has often thought she was born in the wrong era.

In 2004, I watched the wonderful PBS production *Colonial House*, a multipart documentary detailing the lives of several families and individuals committed to spending the summer months on the coast of Maine living exactly as the pilgrims had in the 1600s. As the program began, a master plan was set forth by the appointed leaders, and each individual was assigned a role with specific duties. Some colonists were responsible for planting the corn; others for milking the goats and tending to the chickens. Other colonists had to clear timber, create products for bartering with the Native Americans, and build dwelling structures for families yet to arrive. All women were obliged to work in the kitchen all day, cooking, tending the hearth, and cleaning pots and dishes, meal after meal. These turned out to be the most taxing and strenuous of all the settlement's chores.

The twenty-first century families were soon overwhelmed. They were shocked at how much work it was to simply make it through one day—to provide warmth in the cottage, to put food on the table, to battle the elements of nature (and the native peoples)—and to plan for long-term survival. Each day was a struggle and a game of survival to be won or lost. Several participants dropped out and went home early, unable to cope with the hard work, the lack of food, and the isolation. Others stuck it out, but not without trepidation, complaints, and constant attempts to introduce modern accommodations and mores into their seventeenth-century lives. At the program's conclusion, it was obvious that men and women today, or at least those chosen for the documentary, are not of the same caliber as our tough and determined pilgrim ancestors.

Most members of modern society can hardly fathom the everyday hard work and brutal struggles undertaken by our forefathers and foremothers to lay the foundation of our country. Today, if we need help around the house, we hire handymen and housekeepers. If we want a structure built, we hire a contractor. If we want food, we drive to the supermarket, load up our baskets, and check out with the swipe of a card. For most of us, food is abundant, and the act of procuring it is simple. The thought of food being endangered is absurd. But is it?

Diversity Lost

As the socioeconomic culture shifts and fewer people are willing to do the hard work of growing crops, we are experiencing an ever-increasing homogenization and industrialization of food-production systems and losing much of the genetic diversity of the world's food crops. Large corporations have taken over the responsibility of feeding families, and as a result the variety of crops grown has been streamlined to the most efficient and highest-yielding modern cultivars. We all know that endangered species of animals have been disappearing from the world for decades, but older, open-pollinated plant varieties have also been disappearing from the horticultural landscape, giving way to commercial hybrid varieties. This is a dangerous trend.

The older varieties, many of them brought to the New World by early settlers, represent thousands of years of careful selection and adaptation by farmers, home gardeners, and botanists around the world. Each variety is genetically unique and has developed resistance to the pests and the diseases with which it evolved. Traditionally, horticulturalists use older established varieties to improve modern crops that are constantly being infested by evolving pests and diseases. Without these infusions of genetic diversity, food production is vulnerable to epidemics, and entire crops are subject to extinction.

With so much of our modern plants' genetic material held in patents by large corporations, and with the majority of our food supply coming from these sources, it is in our best interest to save our open-pollinated heirloom seeds and carry on the traditions of our hard-working agrarian ancestors by producing our own food.

Heirlooms Defined

An heirloom plant is defined simply as an open-pollinated cultivar that was commonly grown in earlier periods and has a history of being passed down within a family. Heirlooms are not used in modern large-scale agriculture. An open-pollinated cultivar (as opposed to a hybrid) can be grown from seed and will reproduce true to type. In other words, the second generation of plants will look just like the first. Because we are allowed to save the seeds of open-pollinated cultivars and plant them again the following season, we have the freedom and independence to produce—and reproduce—our own food year after year. In contrast, farmers growing commercial crops are required to purchase seed each year from the corporations holding the patents.

Growing heirloom plants is not done merely to preserve history, nor is it just romantic nostalgia. Heirlooms' wide diversity of types, colors, and flavors allows us to experience food in ways we've never known. With heirloom vegetables, you get purple peppers; tomatoes in shades of green, pink, yellow, orange, and purple; white and red carrots; pink-striped eggplants and orange eggplants; round yellow cucumbers; and many other unusual combinations. Heirlooms not only amuse the eye but also delight the palate with their sweet and succulent variety of vibrant tastes, unlike most of the varieties found in the supermarket, which tend to be bland and homogenous. The latter have been developed not for taste but for good looks and long shelf life so they can withstand the thousands of miles traveled before arriving at their final destinations. What we now consider *heirloom* vegetables and fruit represent those specimens historically selected for superb flavor and intrinsic quality, the seeds of which have been saved and grown year after year.

PRESERVING THE PAST

Increasing numbers of gardeners are beginning to comprehend the scope of our garden heritage and how much of it is in danger of being lost forever. For several decades, there has been a growing movement dedicated to preserving the world's horticultural and culinary history and bringing this pursuit to light. At the forefront of this movement is William Woys Weaver, whose tome *Heirloom Vegetable Gardening* (1997) is exhaustive in its detail about heirloom-variety history and is considered the gold standard for heirloom research. Benjamin Watson is another individual who has compiled much of what is known about the origins of heirloom vegetables in his *Taylor's Guide to Heirloom Vegetables* (1996); many of the historical anecdotes I've included in this book were derived from his research. Groups such as Seed Savers Exchange (SSE) and Slow Food International began quietly heralding the cause many years ago and today have emerged as leaders in the movement to identify and actively preserve our heritage plants and foods.

The nonprofit SSE saves and shares the heirloom seeds representing our garden heritage, thus creating a living legacy to be passed down through generations. Members believe that "when people grow and save seeds, they join an ancient tradition as stewards, nurturing our diverse, fragile, genetic and cultural heritage" (http://www.seedsavers.org). By building a network of folks committed to collecting, conserving, and sharing heirloom seeds and plants, SSE is saving the world's diverse and endangered plant varieties for future generations.

Slow Food International (and Slow Food USA) indicates that we are seeing many traditional food varieties and flavors disappear from the culinary landscape. The spice of Cajun cooking; the traditional methods of Native American and colonial cookery; handcrafted cider, wine, and beer; farmhouse cheeses and other artisanal creations; heritage breeds of livestock; and heirloom varieties of fruits and vegetables—these are all facets of our cultural identity. Slow Food believes such things

reflect generations of commitment to the land and devotion to the processes that yield the greatest achievements in taste. These foods, and the communities that produce and depend on them, are constantly at risk of succumbing to the effects of . . . industrialization and standardization of our food supply and degradation of our farmland. By reviving the pleasures of the table, and using our taste buds as our guides, Slow Food USA believes that our food heritage can be saved. [http://slow food.com]

By educating consumers about food choices beyond supermarkets and fast-food establishments, Slow Food helps to preserve our food traditions and to instill a sense of pride in our national food treasures. As stated on its Web site:

Recognizing that the enjoyment of wholesome food is essential to the pursuit of happiness, Slow Food USA is an educational organization dedicated to stewardship of the land and ecologically sound food production; to the revival of the kitchen and the table as centers of plea-

sure, culture, and community; to the invigoration and proliferation of regional, seasonal culinary traditions; to the creation of a collaborative, ecologically oriented, and virtuous globalization; and to living a slower and more harmonious rhythm of life.

Its mission is succinctly summed up on its Web site as, "Taste, tradition and the honest pleasures of food." With these interests in mind, I arrived at the inspiration for *Cooking with Heirlooms*.

FOOD WITH A STORY

Cooking with Heirlooms is not intended to be a comprehensive text on the history of heirloom plant varieties; it was created with the intention of introducing readers to the delights of heirlooms and providing a few recipes with which to utilize them. (Most recipes will be nearly as tasty if prepared with common varieties of vegetables or fruits.) Some recipes were gathered from heirloom growers around the United States, several of whom are profiled in the text; others were developed by individuals with a passion for cooking with heirlooms.

Some recipes in the book do not use heirloom vegetables and fruits but are heirloom recipes gathered from past generations and enjoyed by the present generation and, it is hoped, by future ones as well. These were added to the book to round out the offerings.

Food with a story is an intriguing topic lately, especially for people who share common interests such as farming, raising livestock, and the traditional ways of our agrarian ancestors. Learning the history of how a particular vegetable variety came into being is a simple way of cherishing the food we grow and put into our bodies every day. By carrying on the work of our ancestors—those who played a hand in creating such diversity—we pay homage to them and perpetuate our vast and bountiful food heritage.

Cooking with Heirlooms is for hobby farmers, kitchen gardeners, homesteaders, foodies, and those who cherish history, particularly food history. It focuses on easily obtainable heirloom varieties—rather than the extremely rare types found only in seed banks—which are cross-referenced to multiple sources and seed companies. Included are some suggestions for which varieties to plant to help you start your own heirloom garden. Please be aware that plant histories are not set in stone; they vary (sometimes greatly) from source to source. Definitive documentation on plant origins is not easy to obtain.

Do It Yourself

If you have never grown heirlooms or saved seeds, begin by purchasing seeds from companies that sell open-pollinated heirloom varieties and that have a commitment to growing their seeds using natural methods (multiple sources are listed in Appendix A). I've spent the last few years experimenting with heirloom varieties, saving seeds, and waiting patiently each season to see what will reproduce. I've kept a garden journal to track my pursuits and to determine what worked and what didn't. I've always been advised to grow what I like, so I've invested in multiple varieties of tomatoes, melons, squashes, and herbs.

Each season I marvel that planting a seed the size of a flea during the cold, early days of spring results in flowers giving way to developing fruits a few short months later. Before I know it, I'm in my kitchen creating fresh salsas and sauces, grilled zucchini and zucchini bread, and herbal concoctions from those once nearly imperceptible seeds. Preserving the fresh fruits from my garden extends my pleasure and has taught me the intrinsic value of eating in season. Our ancestors had no choice but to eat in season, and embracing heirlooms will forever make you think twice about grabbing apples from the grocery store in May, asparagus in December, or tomatoes during any month of the year!

Expand your garden selections yearly, and each harvest you'll feel pride in the work you're doing on behalf of seed preservation. You'll also learn of at least one new pest each year and develop tactics to prevent it from robbing you of your garden treasures.

Through heirloom gardening and cooking, you can reconnect with the traditional American values of our hardworking seventeenth-century colonists—self-sustainability, independence, and freedom—and join the legion of passionate heirloom gardeners and chefs around the world.

SPRING

 Spring marks the beginning of a farmer's busy year, when outdoor activity commences. For most growers, it is truly the most glorious season for a single reason—it's the end of winter. Eager gardeners revel in those first warm and sunny days, but winter doesn't release its grasp easily; wet, cold, and stormy days still lie ahead. The savvy hobby farmer must watch the forecasts, plan wisely, and not be fooled into premature planting.

The flurry of early garden activity includes weeding, bed preparation, and when the time is right, planting. Before long, we're harvesting the first fresh herbs and vegetables of the year: asparagus, lettuce greens, radishes, the tiny sweet fruits of strawberry plants, and the meaty stalks of rhubarb. The hobby farm kitchen is also revitalized as the heavy, starchy winter fare gives way to herb-laced spring salads, fresh lamb shanks, and rhubarb cobbler.

THE BOYCE FAMILY

HEIRLOOM GROWER **SHADY ELM FARM**

or Doug and Amanda Boyce and family, growing and cooking with heirloom vegetables has become a way of life. In 1998, while living in an apartment in Wisconsin, the couple attended a garden expo in Madison, where they learned about heirloom varieties and saving seeds. From that moment, they were hooked. Amanda began saving seeds from her heirloom Amish Paste tomatoes, and she's expanded her efforts every year since.

Today, Doug and Amanda operate their five-acre Shady Elm Farm, in Spring Valley, Wisconsin, as a part-time endeavor. While Doug works from home as a software developer and consultant, Amanda keeps track of their three boys, Josiah, Marcus, and Jayden, and takes care of the daily chores associated with managing a farm. They have two acres dedicated to intensive vegetable production, consisting of about 95 percent heirloom varieties. Twenty-one varieties of vegetables and herbs—such as French Fingerling potatoes, Lollo Rosso lettuce, Mammoth Red Rock cabbage, and Dark Purple Opal basil—provide their community supported agriculture (CSA) customers with fresh produce baskets from June to October. (A CSA farm involves consumers buying "shares" of a local farm prior to the growing season. During the growing season, "members" then receive weekly shares—a basket of fresh produce—directly from the farmer.)

During the first year of operating their CSA in 2004, the Boyces started small to get used to the direct marketing of produce gradually as their knowledge and family grew. Today this aspect of farming has turned out to be the most satisfying for them. "The people who are interested [in subscribing to a CSA] already have a little knowledge about eating in-season produce and love fresh food," says Amanda. "They are curious and open to new varieties of vegetables and love it when you give them new food ideas." Although business has been so good for the Boyces that they could expand more rapidly, they have wisely limited the number of shares to what they feel they can handle well. They don't want to sacrifice quality or service, and they still want to enjoy the work without being run ragged.

In addition to their garden crops, the Boyces raise a varied flock of laying hens on pasture—including Araucanas, Silver-Laced Wyandottes, and Speckled Sussex—and cockerels for meat during the summer months. They've found heritage breeds of livestock, like heirloom vegetables, to be more adaptable and hardier. Doug and Amanda plan to add either Shetland or Icelandic sheep to their farm in the near future for colored fleece and for weed control. "Heritage breeds seem to fit our needs on a small farm better than the more common breeds found on larger farms, and we love the diversity [they bring] to our lives," says Amanda.

Although Doug and Amanda both have their cooking specialties (Doug is the baker and Amanda loves to make holiday treats), it is Amanda who prepares the daily meals with in-season produce in the spring, the summer, and the fall and who preserves as much as possible for the winter months. The typical summer meal preparation begins with heading out to the garden and identifying what is ready to harvest that day. Amanda uses heirloom varieties almost exclusively for all of her dishes, feeling that they offer a larger palette of color and subtle differences in flavor that make each recipe unique. Having grown up on a dairy farm where homemade meals were cooked from memory, not recipe cards, Amanda prefers this way of cooking herself. "Certainly, there are some basics to be learned in cooking, but it is fun to see how much variety a person can make from just a few garden ingredients," she says.

Farming has allowed the Boyce family to reconnect with the basics of life. "When we grow our own raw ingredients and learn to make them into useful things, we find satisfaction," says Amanda. "Passing these things on to the next generation is a priority for us, and working together with the natural world by farming the land is a great blessing."

Sample Amanda's cooking by preparing her Spring Herb Salad on page 50, Summer Raspberry Cheesecake on page 123, or Grandma Beach's Marinated Carrots on page 160.

Shady Elm Farm
N8726 50th St.
Spring Valley, WI 54767
(715) 772-4599
http://www.shadyelmfarm.com

SPRING HERB SOUP

Spring Herb Soup

This simple, flavorful soup carries on the centuries-old tradition of using the newly sprouted herbs of spring as a health-boosting tonic.

YIELD: 4 TO 6 SERVINGS

1 tablespoon canola or olive oil

1 cup finely chopped celery

¼ cup minced fresh heirloom chives, such as Chinese or garlic chives

¼ cup minced fresh heirloom sorrel, such as common garden sorrel or French sorrel

2 tablespoons minced fresh chervil leaves

2 tablespoons minced fresh tarragon leaves

6 cups vegetable broth

Pinch of sugar

Salt and ground black pepper, to taste

4 to 6 slices whole wheat bread, toasted and crusts trimmed

½ to ¾ cup grated Monterey Jack cheese

Grated nutmeg

❖ In a large dutch oven, warm the oil over medium heat. Add the celery and herbs, and cook, stirring occasionally, about 3 to 5 minutes or until wilted and soft. Add the broth, sugar, salt, and pepper. Bring to a boil, and reduce heat to low. Cover and simmer for 20 minutes.

Place a slice of toast in each soup bowl, and sprinkle with 2 tablespoons grated cheese and a dusting of nutmeg. Pour the soup over the top.

Spinach- and Sausage-Stuffed Mushrooms

YIELD: 20 APPETIZERS

20 large button mushrooms

4 tablespoons olive oil

Salt and pepper, to taste

¼ cup finely chopped white onion

½ tablespoon minced garlic

½ cup finely diced chicken-apple sausage

½ teaspoon red pepper flakes

¼ teaspoon dried thyme

2 cups chopped fresh heirloom spinach, such as Bloomsdale Long Standing

¼ cup plain breadcrumbs

3 tablespoons heavy cream

¼ cup grated Parmesan cheese

❖ Heat a large skillet with olive oil over medium heat; sauté the onion and garlic until soft. Add the chicken-apple sausage, and brown slightly. Add the red pepper flakes, thyme, and spinach. When the spinach is wilted, mix in the breadcrumbs and heavy cream. Reduce the cream, and season as needed.

Using a tablespoon, mound the hot mixture into the mushroom caps, and sprinkle with the cheese. Return to the oven, and heat until the cheese has melted, about 6 to10 minutes.

Onion Soup

Fix this toasty onion soup on a chilly spring day after working outside. It's quick and easy, and you probably have everything you need in your pantry right now.

YIELD: 4 SERVINGS

2 medium-size heirloom onions, such as Yellow Globe
   Danvers
2 ounces butter
1 quart beef stock
⅔ cup dry sherry
Salt and pepper, to taste
5 slices bread, toasted
¼ cup grated sharp cheese

❖ Chop the onions finely. Heat the butter in a dutch oven. Add the onions and sauté until tender. Add the stock and the sherry and bring to a boil. Season the soup with salt and pepper to taste. Cube the toasted bread.

Serve the soup in bowls garnished with bread cubes and grated cheese.

HEIRLOOM:
YELLOW GLOBE DANVERS ONION

Known also as Yellow Danvers, this medium-size round yellow onion originated in England and was introduced to America in the nineteenth century. It is thought to have first been grown around Danvers, Massachusetts (hence, its name), before 1850. It has brownish yellow skin; yellow fine-grained flesh; and a good, strong onion flavor. The Yellow Danvers onion is a popular variety with heirloom gardeners as well as gourmands.

Chilled Borscht

Acidic ingredients, such as the vinegar and lemon juice used in this recipe, will heighten the ruby red color of beets. Be sure to choose beets with green, healthy tops and no signs of yellowing; a deep, even color in the beetroot; a firm globular shape; and smooth unblemished skin free of punctures. Beets cooked shortly after harvest are sweeter and less tough than stored beets.

YIELD: 6 SERVINGS

2 pounds medium-size heirloom beets, such as Detroit Dark Red, scrubbed and stems removed

1 small onion, peeled and cut in half

7 cups water

¼ cup white vinegar

¼ cup sugar

Salt, to taste

¾ cup heavy cream

¾ cup sour cream

2 tablespoons lemon juice

2 tablespoons chopped fresh dill

❖ Place the beets, onion, water, vinegar, sugar, and salt in a large saucepan. Bring to a boil over high heat. Reduce the heat to medium low, cover partially, and simmer about 45 minutes or until the beets are tender.

Remove and discard the onion. Move the beets to a cutting board, and let cool slightly. Strain the liquid, and reserve.

Remove the skin from the beets. Coarsely grate half the beets; refrigerate until cold. Cut the remaining beets into large chunks. Place half of the chunks in a blender. Add just enough cooking liquid to cover them, and blend until very smooth, about 2 minutes. Transfer this mixture to a large container. Repeat with the remaining beet chunks. Stir the remaining cooking liquid into the pureed beets, and refrigerate until cold, about 2 hours.

Remove the pureed beets and the grated beets from the refrigerator. Whisk the heavy cream and sour cream into the pureed beets until smooth and fully blended. Stir in the grated beets. Stir in the lemon juice, and adjust the seasonings. Ladle the soup into bowls, and garnish with the dill. Serve immediately.

HEIRLOOM: DETROIT DARK RED BEET

Developed from the popular European Early Blood Turnip beet, Detroit Dark Red was introduced in America in 1892. Now widely adapted and considered the standard for beets, this heirloom has dark red flesh and globe-shaped roots. It is tender, sweet, and smooth tasting, and its dark green foliage is as tasty as chard or spinach. These beets are good for eating fresh, canning, and pickling. Detroit Dark Reds are ideal for summer or fall harvest, and they are excellent keepers.

CHILLED BORSCHT

Hummus

This homemade dish is infinitely better than any store-bought variety and worth the effort. Serve it with toasted pita bread or a variety of vegetables such as carrots, zucchini, celery, radishes, and cherry tomatoes.

‖|‖

YIELD: 3 CUPS

¾ pound dried garbanzo beans

Pinch of baking soda

1 teaspoon salt

½ cup sesame tahini

8 cloves garlic, such as Spanish Roja, peeled and minced

6 to 9 tablespoons fresh lemon juice, divided

2 to 3 tablespoons extra-virgin olive oil

❖ Soak the beans overnight in cool water with a pinch of baking soda. If you want to reduce the cooking time, you may soak them for up to three days in the refrigerator, but change the water daily.

After soaking, drain and rinse the beans. Place the beans in a large saucepan with enough salted water to cover them by ½ inch. Simmer the beans until they are very soft, which can take 2 hours. Be sure to keep the water level up in the pot while cooking. When they are done, drain, rinse, and set aside.

Put the beans, tahini, garlic, and 5 tablespoons of lemon juice in the bowl of a food processor. Pulse until the beans are ground to a fine paste. Add more salt and more lemon juice, if needed, and up to 3 tablespoons olive oil to achieve the desired texture and flavor. Chill before serving to meld flavors. Adjust seasonings if needed.

HEIRLOOM:
SPANISH ROJA GARLIC

There are two types of garlic: hardneck and softneck. There are five varieties, with Rocambole being the most widely grown of the hardnecks. Rocamboles produce large cloves that are easily peeled, making them preferred by cooks and chefs everywhere. Their loose skins, however, contribute to their major disadvantage—a shorter storage life than that of most other varieties. By midwinter, most Rocamboles show signs of dehydration or begin to sprout. Curing the bulbs well before storage will extend their shelf life.

Spanish Roja, a Rocambole strain, was first brought to the Portland area by Greek immigrants in the late 1800s. Its clove color varies with soil and climate; it can be light to dark brown with a red-purple blush. When grown well, Spanish Roja has a deep, full-bodied, classic garlic taste.

Heirloom Potato Soup with Roasted Garlic and Caramelized Onions

YIELD: 4 TO 6 SERVINGS

2 large bulbs heirloom garlic, such as Spanish Roja, roasted

2 tablespoons extra-virgin olive oil

3 medium onions, thinly sliced

4 cups vegetable or chicken broth

¾ pound heirloom potatoes, such as Early Rose, peeled and chopped

1½ teaspoons dried sage

2 teaspoons chopped fresh thyme leaves

1 teaspoon chopped fresh rosemary leaves

1 tablespoon fresh lemon juice

Salt and pepper, to taste

❖ Preheat the oven to 375°F.

To roast the garlic, peel the outer skins off the bulbs until the clove skins are visible. Place the bulbs on a piece of foil, and lightly drizzle with olive oil. Wrap tightly and roast 40 to 45 minutes or until soft; cool and peel.

Heat the olive oil in a small skillet and add the onion. Cook the onion over medium heat 10 to 15 minutes or until browned and caramelized. Remove from the heat.

Heat the broth in a stockpot; add the chopped potatoes. Simmer 15 to 20 minutes or until the potatoes are tender. Stir in the onion and roasted garlic; simmer for 10 minutes to blend the flavors. Just before serving, season with the herbs, lemon juice, and salt and pepper.

HEIRLOOM: EARLY ROSE POTATO

An old American heirloom introduced in 1861, the Early Rose potato has a smooth pinkish red skin, deep-set eyes, and delicious white flesh streaked with red. Early Rose potatoes were economically successful for farmers in the late nineteenth century, and the variety was grown under twenty-four aliases, including Antwerp, Boston Market, and Watson's Seedling. Wealthy European aristocrats grew Early Rose potatoes in the late 1800s, a time when they maintained greenhouses year-round to grow whatever was unavailable at the markets; they deemed this variety the best potato for growing in a hothouse culture.

Western Eggs

Serve this dish simply with wheat toast, and you'll have a satisfying breakfast before a long day of farm chores.

‖♦‖

YIELD: 6 SERVINGS

4 bacon slices

2 small green bell peppers, seeded and chopped

1 small onion, chopped

1 clove garlic, minced

2 tomatoes, seeded and chopped

Salt and pepper, to taste

12 large farmstead eggs, beaten

¼ cup cream

4 tablespoons butter

❖ Cook the bacon in a large skillet until crisp. Remove the bacon, and crumble. Save 2 tablespoons of the bacon fat, and discard the rest. Sauté the pepper, onion, and garlic in the bacon fat until tender. Add the tomatoes and sauté for 1 minute.

Combine the eggs and cream in a small bowl. Pour over the vegetables, and add salt and pepper to taste. Stir the egg mixture until the eggs are cooked.

FARMSTEAD EGGS

Farmstead eggs are eggs from chickens raised outdoors in small hobby flocks. Farmstead eggs aren't necessarily organic because hens usually get tossed kitchen scraps and various leftovers. However, their eggs taste better than eggs from commercial flocks because the birds are raised naturally, and they eat protein sources such as bugs and seeds. Fresh farmstead eggs have brilliant yellow round yolks with intense yolky flavor; the whites are thick and dense and stick together. The latter makes a difference in recipes, such as angel food cake or meringue, that call for the whites to provide structure, but the quality is even evident in a simple fried egg. Store-bought eggs are usually four to six weeks old at the time of purchase and thus stale. Their flavor is bland, and the whole egg seems to lose its shape when cracked into a pan for frying.

WESTERN EGGS

Crunchy Omelet

❙❙❙

YIELD: 6 TO 8 SERVINGS

4 slices whole grain brown bread

4 tablespoons butter or margarine, divided

1 tablespoon chopped green onion tops

2 tablespoons minced shallot

2 teaspoons coarsely chopped fresh leaf parsley

½ cup pitted and chopped green and black olives (optional)

15 large farmstead eggs

¼ cup cream or milk

1 teaspoon Chinese 5-Spice powder or Mrs. Dash's natural
     seasoning

½ cup grated mixed cheeses, such as Swiss, sharp cheddar,
     Monterey Jack

❖ Heat a platter. Cut the bread into 1-inch cubes, and sauté in 3 tablespoons of the butter. Add the green onion and shallot, and continue sautéing until cubes are golden. Toss with the parsley and set aside. Add the olives, if desired.

In a large bowl, whip the eggs with the cream. Add the spice and mix well.

Add the remaining butter to a heated nonstick skillet on medium-low heat, and melt carefully. Pour in the egg mixture and cook slowly, lifting edges of eggs and letting liquid flow from center to edges until mostly set. When center is still moist but edges are set, add most of the cheese and the bread cube mixture. Fold over, and slip omelet onto a heated platter. Sprinkle with the remaining grated cheese. Serve immediately, cutting slices at the table.

Garnish with fresh fruit and serve with garlic biscuits and honey.

Carrot-Nut Bread

Carrots taste best when eaten shortly after harvest, in cool weather.

YIELD: 4 TO 6 SERVINGS

1½ cups unbleached all-purpose flour, sifted

1 cup whole wheat flour, sifted

1 teaspoon baking soda

2½ teaspoons baking powder

1 teaspoon salt

¾ cup packed light brown sugar

1 cup milk

2 large farmstead eggs

2 tablespoons butter, melted

1 cup grated heirloom carrots, such as Chantenay

½ cup chopped pecans or walnuts

❖ Preheat the oven to 375°F. Lightly grease and flour a 4 x 8–inch loaf pan.

Combine the flours, baking soda, baking powder, salt, and brown sugar in a large bowl. Mix well. Pour the milk into a medium bowl, and add the eggs and butter. Mix well. Stir the milk mixture into the dry ingredients, mixing well. Fold in the carrots and nuts.

Pour the batter into the prepared pan. Bake 1 hour or until a wooden pick placed in the center of the loaf comes cut clean. Remove from the oven, and let cool in pan until the loaf moves away from the sides of the pan. Remove from the pan, and cool completely on wire rack.

Serve warm with butter or cream cheese.

HEIRLOOM: CHANTENAY CARROT

The earliest known carrots originated in Afghanistan and were purple and yellow in color. The orange carrots we know today were first developed in Holland in the 1600s and bred enthusiastically by the French in the 1800s. The Chantenay variety was devel-

oped in France in the 1830s and made its way to America in the late 1800s. Chantenays are large, tender, and sweet, becoming even sweeter in storage. This multiuse variety is well suited for the table, canning, freezing, juicing, and storing.

Sugar-Topped Apple Muffins

YIELD: 12 TO 15 MUFFINS

4 tablespoons shortening

½ cup plus 2 tablespoons sugar, divided

1 large farmstead egg, beaten

2 cups sifted unbleached all-purpose flour

3½ teaspoons baking powder

½ teaspoon salt

1 teaspoon cinnamon, divided

1 cup milk

2 cups peeled and chopped heirloom apples, such as
   Baldwin

1 cup crushed corn flakes

½ cup chopped pecans

❖ Preheat the oven to 400°F. Grease the inside of a muffin tin.

Cream the shortening and the ½ cup sugar in a medium bowl. Add the egg, mixing well.

Combine the flour, baking powder, salt, and ½ teaspoon of the cinnamon in a large bowl. Alternate between adding the flour mixture and the milk into the shortening mixture as you stir. Stir just enough to mix the ingredients. Fold in the apples, corn flakes, and pecans.

Spoon the batter into the prepared muffin tin, filling it two-thirds full. Combine the remaining sugar and cinnamon in a small bowl. Sprinkle over the batter.

Bake 25 minutes or until lightly golden. Serve warm.

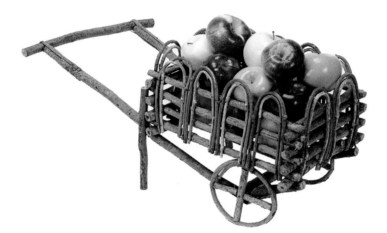

Rhubarb, Strawberry, and Hazelnut Scones

From spring through early summer, rhubarb grows in abundance. Its fleshy red and green stalks make delicious preserves, sauces, crisps, and cobblers, particularly when paired with strawberries to sweeten their sour taste. For those living in colder climates, the arrival of rhubarb is a harbinger of spring. A freshly baked pie or batch of scones can raise our spirits after a long, cold winter. *Cooks heed caution: rhubarb leaves are poisonous.*

YIELD: 8 SERVINGS

2 cups whole wheat flour

1 tablespoon baking powder

1 teaspoon salt

2 tablespoons unsalted butter

4 tablespoons honey

½ cup whole milk

1½ cups heavy cream

1 large farmstead egg, beaten

1 cup diced fresh heirloom rhubarb, such as Victoria

2 cups diced strawberries

½ cup chopped hazelnuts, toasted*

❖ Preheat the oven to 375°F.

Combine the flour, baking powder, and salt in a large bowl. Cut in the butter until well mixed. Stir in the honey, milk, heavy cream, and egg. Mix well. Fold in the rhubarb, strawberries, and hazelnuts. Pour batter in ½-cup measurements onto an ungreased baking sheet. Bake 20 minutes or until golden.

Serve this dessert topped with double cream and chopped strawberries.

* To toast hazelnuts, place an even layer in a small, dry frying pan. Toss over high heat for 1 to 2 minutes until toasted. Be careful not to burn.

VEGETARIAN LINGUINE CARBONARA

Vegetarian Linguine Carbonara

Many ingredients can be added to this dish to give you a different meal each time you serve it—it's great with a tossed salad, fresh bread, and a good light dry red wine such as a pinot noir. If you would like to add some meat, it can be made the traditional way with pancetta or a good dry-cured natural bacon.

YIELD: 4 TO 6 SERVINGS

1 pound linguine pasta

2 tablespoons extra-virgin olive oil

1 cup fresh heirloom spinach, such as Bloomsdale Long
   Standing

1 tablespoon dried or 3 tablespoons chopped fresh basil

¼ teaspoon red pepper flakes

Salt and freshly ground black pepper, to taste

1 whole bulb garlic, minced

¼ cup extra-virgin olive oil

2 large farmstead eggs

Fresh Parmesan cheese, grated

❖ Cook the linguine according to the package directions. Drain linguine, and place back in pot. Add 2 tablespoons olive oil and the spinach, basil, red pepper flakes, salt, and pepper. Toss the mixture, keeping the pot on low heat.

In a small skillet, sauté the minced garlic in ¼ cup olive oil over medium to low heat for 1 to 2 minutes, watching carefully so it doesn't burn. Add the garlic mixture to the linguine, and toss well.

Whisk the eggs in a small bowl, and add them to the linguine mixture. Using tongs, toss the mixture until the egg s cooked and mixed well. (If the egg makes the pasta clump, add 1 more tablespoon of oil to the mixture.)

Place the pasta on a serving platter, and top with a sprinkling of fresh Parmesan cheese.

(Optional toppings include toasted pine nuts, feta cheese, minced kalamata olives, and oven-roasted bell peppers.)

White Chili

Serve this chicken chili with crusty sourdough bread and garlic butter on the side.

‖♦‖

YIELD: 4 SERVINGS

1 pound dried Great Northern beans or other heirloom dry white beans

2 cups organic vegetable broth

2 cups organic free-range chicken broth

2 medium sweet onions, chopped

4 cloves garlic, minced

1 teaspoon seasoning salt

2 tablespoons Worcestershire sauce

½ cup diced fresh green chilies

2 teaspoons ground cumin

1½ teaspoons dried oregano

¼ teaspoon cayenne pepper

½ teaspoon red pepper flakes

½ pound grilled or roasted chicken breasts, cut into ¼-inch strips

1 cup grated Monterey Jack cheese

Sour cream

❖ Place the beans in a large stockpot, cover with water, and soak overnight. Drain and rinse with cold water. Return the beans to the stockpot, and add the vegetable and chicken broth, 2 cups of the chopped onions, the garlic, and the seasoning salt. Bring to a boil, then reduce the heat, cover, and simmer gently for 1½ to 2 hours or until the beans are very tender. Add more stock if needed during cooking. Stir in the Worcestershire sauce, the remaining seasonings, and the remaining onions. Cover, and cook for 30 minutes. Just before serving, add the chicken and cook until heated.

Serve in individual bowls. Top each with grated cheese and a dollop of sour cream.

HEIRLOOM:
GREAT NORTHERN BEAN

The colors, shapes, and sizes of the hundreds of varieties of heirloom beans in their dry, mature stage are astounding. Like little works of art, all with unique and interesting histories, beans represent some of the most varied and hard to define crops. Snap beans, pole beans, runner beans, fava beans (broad beans), and lima beans—they all belong to the same species, but each has different characteristics.

The Great Northern white bean, a very old variety, is used both as a shelling bean and a dry bean. It was originally grown by the Mandan Indians of the Dakotas. Great Northerns are larger than the common navy bean and cook more quickly. This variety is fairly common today and is available in many grocery stores.

Steak with Blue Cheese and Sun-Dried Tomato Butter

YIELD: 4 SERVINGS

1 pound unsalted whipped butter, softened

¼ cup finely chopped sun-dried tomatoes

1 teaspoon finely chopped fresh oregano

2 tablespoons crumbled blue cheese

4 grass-fed beef steaks (porterhouse, rib eye, T-bone, or New York strip)

❖ Whip the butter in a medium bowl until smooth. Fold the sun-dried tomatoes, oregano, and blue cheese into the butter. Lay the mixture in a thick line lengthwise on parchment paper, and roll into a log or tube shape that's about 6 to 8 inches long (make sure to roll the parchment tight and not to overlap the parchment into the mixture). Twist the parchment closed on the ends, and wrap tightly with plastic wrap. Place in the freezer for 1 hour or until firm. Unwrap the mixture and slice into pats.

Grill meat until it reaches an internal temperature between 135° to 165°F, according to your preference. Remove from grill, and allow to sit for 5 to 10 minutes. Top with a few pats of the butter mixture just before serving.

Serve grilled steaks with a salad and crusty Italian bread spread with the leftover prepared butter mixture.

HEIRLOOM:
HERITAGE GRASS-FED BEEF

Heritage cattle—endangered or older breeds such as the Devon, the Highland, and the Galloway—are most often grass fed and raised on small family farms. Grass-fed cattle eat what they would naturally eat in the wild—not corn, antibiotics, and hormones. They are in a constant state of movement, always seeking fresh green forage. As a result of the cattle's diet and exercise, grass-fed beef is lower in fat and calories and higher in vitamin E and heart-healthy omega-3 fatty acids. The meat from animals that are raised on pasture is very distinct and incredibly flavorful, so it does not need to be overly doctored with seasonings and sauces.

ROASTED FISH IN A NUT CRUST

Roasted Fish in a Nut Crust

Serve this fragrant, crunchy fish with homemade tartar sauce, lime and lemon wedges, and an heirloom spinach salad.

YIELD: 4 TO 6 SERVINGS

½ cup finely chopped toasted walnuts, pecans, or macadamia nuts

½ cup dry white breadcrumbs

¼ cup minced fresh lemon thyme or 2 tablespoons dried thyme

1 tablespoon freshly minced or grated lime or lemon zest

2 large farmstead eggs

1 cup whole milk

2 pounds white fish filets (such as red snapper, tilapia, or orange roughy) at least 1 inch thick, skinned and cut into 8 equal pieces

Seasoning salt

Freshly ground black pepper

¾ cup melted unsalted butter or ½ cup olive oil

1 teaspoon grated fresh lemon or lime zest

Fresh thyme or other herb sprigs for garnish

❖ Preheat the oven to 550°F.

Cover a baking sheet with parchment paper brushed with oil or use a baking rack brushed with oil on the baking sheet.

In a shallow bowl or pan combine the nuts, breadcrumbs, thyme, and zest, and set aside. In another shallow bowl or pan, beat the eggs, add milk, and set aside.

Rinse the fish under running water, and pat dry with paper towels. Season with salt and pepper to taste. Dip each piece of fish into the milk and egg mixture and then into the nut mixture to cover completely. Pat each piece firmly so nut mixture will adhere.

Arrange the fish so they don't touch on the prepared rack, or place each piece on the parchment paper. Drizzle the melted butter or oil over the fish.

Bake the fish on the top oven rack until they are golden on the outside and they flake when pierced in the center with the tip of a sharp knife, about 10 minutes per inch of thickness.

Transfer the fish pieces to a warmed platter, and garnish with the fresh herbs and zest.

Lamb Shanks with Herbs and Caramelized Onions

Spring is the time when fresh, succulent lamb is available on your farm, at the farmers' market, or at the butcher shop. Prepare this dish for Sunday supper with yellow heirloom onions, such as Yellow Globe Danvers or Ebenezer, which will provide a hearty, pungent flavor.

YIELD: 6 SERVINGS

1 cup unbleached all-purpose flour

½ teaspoon salt

½ teaspoon freshly ground pepper

6 lamb shanks, each sawed into 2-inch lengths

3 tablespoons extra-virgin olive oil

6 yellow onions, thinly sliced

4 large cloves garlic, minced

¼ cup chopped fresh flat-leaf parsley

2 teaspoons fresh minced oregano

3 sprigs fresh rosemary

3 cups vegetable broth

1 cup dry red wine (such as cabernet sauvignon or Shiraz)

❖ Combine the flour, salt, and pepper, and dredge the lamb in the mixture, shaking off excess.

In a dutch oven, heat the oil over medium-high heat; add lamb to the pot, browning on all sides, about 7 to 8 minutes. Remove the meat and set aside.

Add the onions and garlic to the pot, and cook until the onions have softened. Place the browned lamb shanks on top of the onions; add the parsley, oregano, rosemary, vegetable broth, and wine; and bring to a boil. Reduce heat, cover, and simmer for 1½ to 2 hours.

Remove the lamb and rosemary sprigs from the pan, and discard the rosemary. Once sauce is cool, skim off fat and oil, and puree the onions and sauce in a food processor. Return the sauce to the pan, and simmer for about 5 minutes. Adjust the seasonings, pour the sauce over the meat, and serve.

Everyday Pasta

This dish is the essence of Italian farmhouse cooking. It can be prepared differently throughout the year with each season's best heirloom vegetables.

❦

YIELD: 4 SERVINGS

2 to 3 tablespoons olive oil

2 or 3 boneless, skinless chicken breasts, cut into 1-inch pieces

1 teaspoon or more minced garlic

1 tablespoon dried basil or ¼ cup minced fresh basil

1 to 2 teaspoons mixed fresh or dry herbs (such as oregano, parsley, marjoram, or a pinch of thyme)

Salt and pepper, to taste

2 to 3 cups mixed fresh heirloom vegetables, such as asparagus, carrots, greens

1 medium red or yellow heirloom onion, such as Red Wethersfield or Yellow Ebenezer

3 tablespoons cooking sherry or white cooking wine

½ to 1 pound tagliatelle, fusilli, penne, orecchiette, or farfalle pasta, cooked al dente

❖ Heat the olive oil in a 10- or 12-inch skillet over medium-high heat. Sauté the chicken and garlic until the chicken is just starting to turn white. Add basil, the other herbs, salt, and pepper. Cook 2 minutes. Start adding the heirloom vegetables, starting with the ones that take longer to cook (such as carrots). Add the sherry after a few minutes. Continue to cook the chicken and vegetables until tender. Remove from the stove, and toss with the cooked pasta. Serve immediately with a little Parmigiano-Reggiano or fresh goat cheese.

Spring Fried Rice

❦

YIELD: 4 SERVINGS

4 mushrooms, sliced

½ carrot, grated

1 green onion, finely chopped

2 tablespoons peanut or olive oil

2 tablespoons soy sauce

2 cups cooked brown rice, chilled

2 cups cooked white rice, chilled

1 large farmstead egg, beaten

½ cup roasted mixed nuts, chopped

❖ In a wok or large nonstick skillet heated to medium low, sauté the mushrooms, carrot, and onion in the oil and soy sauce until the onion becomes translucent. Add the rice and mix well. Increase the heat to medium high, add the beaten egg, and continue frying, tossing the mixture with a wooden spoon. When the egg is cooked and the mixture is slightly browned on edges of rice, remove from the heat. Toss the mixture with roasted nuts, and serve in small bowls with soy sauce on the side.

Rosemary and Feta Roast Chicken

YIELD: 4 TO 6 SERVINGS

1 5-pound free-range roasting chicken

Dash of olive oil

½ cup feta cheese

¼ cup chopped rosemary

1 teaspoon oregano

1 teaspoon dried basil

1 tablespoon sun-dried tomatoes, soaked and chopped into very fine pieces

5 sprigs rosemary

Salt and black pepper, to taste

GRAVY

Juice from the rosemary and feta roast chicken roasting pan

½ cup water

1 to 2 pinches of chicken bouillon (optional)

2 small pinches of unbleached all-purpose flour

❖ Preheat the oven to 350°F.

Remove the giblets from the chicken, rinse the chicken well, and pat dry. Rub with a dash of olive oil. Place in a roasting pan, breast side down. Rub a dash of olive oil over the breast.

Combine the feta cheese, chopped rosemary, oregano, basil, and chopped sun-dried tomatoes in a medium bowl.

Sliver the skin of the chicken every 2 inches or so. In each cut, insert about 1 teaspoon of the mixture until it is gone. Place the rosemary stalks in the chicken cavity. Salt and pepper the chicken, to taste.

Roast the chicken uncovered for 2 hours, basting often. To prevent the skin from overbrowning, you may need to cover areas, especially the wings and the legs, with foil. The chicken is done when the leg or the wing moves easily in the socket.

Let stand on a serving platter for about 5 minutes before slicing.

GRAVY

Pour the juice from the roasting pan through a strainer into a saucepan. Add water. For more intense flavor, add a pinch or two of chicken bouillon. Simmer on low heat, slowly stirring in two small pinches of flour. Stir until thickened to the consistency you desire. Add salt and pepper to taste.

Louisiana Jambalaya

This traditional southern dish is a filling, delicious supper when spring temperatures haven't yet turned the corner.

YIELD: 12 SERVINGS

4 tablespoons butter

2 cups diced heirloom yellow or white onion, such as Ailsa Craig Exhibition or Southport White Globe

2 cups chopped celery

1½ cups chopped green pepper

3 cloves garlic, minced

1 28-ounce can diced tomatoes in juice

1 tablespoon Worcestershire sauce

1 tablespoon Cajun seasoning

2 teaspoons salt

1 pound smoked sausage, thinly sliced

3 cups cooked rice

5 cups chicken stock

2 pounds small cooked or raw shrimp, peeled and thawed

1 bunch green onions, thinly sliced

½ bunch fresh parsley, chopped

Hot sauce, to taste

❖ In a large dutch oven, melt the butter over medium heat. Add the onion, celery, green pepper, and garlic. Cook 5 to 10 minutes or until tender. Add the diced tomatoes, Worcestershire sauce, Cajun seasoning, and salt. Simmer 10 minutes. Add the sausage and rice, stirring until well mixed. Add the chicken stock, stirring well. Bring to a boil then turn heat to low, cover, and simmer for 15 minutes. Add the shrimp, and gently heat until warm. Add the green onions and parsley. Season with hot sauce to taste.

Fish and Sugar Snap Peas in Foil

This dish is perfect to prepare with the first fresh peas of the season in early June. The peas and pods of snap peas are eaten when their pods are thick and swollen and the peas are sweet. Sugar snap peas require very little cooking, so be mindful of overcook ng—if the pods soften, the flavor is destroyed. Sugar snap peas have strings along the seam that can be removed before eating. To do this, pinch the end of the pea and take hold of the string. Pull the string up the straightest side toward the stem end, pinch off the stem end, and continue pulling the string until it's free.

YIELD: 6 SERVINGS

Cooking spray

½ teaspoon kosher salt

¼ teaspoon freshly ground pepper

2 tablespoons butter, cut into 12 very thin slices

6 8-ounce white fish (such as sea bass or halibut) fillets, at
   least 1 inch thick

6 to 12 basil leaves

4 tablespoons finely chopped shallots

1 cup sugar snap peas

18 baby carrots, trimmed

1 lemon, sliced into 6 thin rounds

12 sprigs fresh thyme or lemon thyme

6 tablespoons dry white wine

❖ Preheat the oven to 400°F.

Cut six 9 × 12–inch pieces of aluminum foil. Combine the salt and pepper in a small bowl.

Place the pieces of the foil on a work surface. Spray the foil with cooking spray, and place two pats of butter in the center of each piece of foil. Place a fish fillet on the butter, place one or two basil leaves on each fillet, and season lightly with salt and pepper. Sprinkle each fillet with 2 teaspoons of the shallots. Top with about 3 tablespoons of the peas, 3 baby carrots, 1 lemon slice, and 2 sprigs of thyme. Then sprinkle with 1 tablespoon of the wine.

Fold the foil over each fillet to enclose the fish and vegetables, and tightly fold the ends closed to make a packet. (The packets can be prepared up to 4 hours ahead and refrigerated.) Place the packets on two large baking sheets. Bake 15 to 20 minutes. Transfer the contents of each packet to a dinner plate, and serve immediately.

Beef Stew

Prepare this easy spring stew with heirloom vegetables you've stored from the fall such as Bintje potatoes and Scarlet Nantes carrots, both of which keep well through a long season. Use mild and sweet yellow onions such as Yellow Ebenezer or Yellow Sweet Spanish.

YIELD: 6 TO 8 SERVINGS

¼ cup unbleached all-purpose flour

¼ teaspoon celery seed

1¼ teaspoons salt

⅛ teaspoon black pepper

2 pounds stewing beef, cut into 1-inch cubes

4 medium onions, coarsely chopped

6 medium potatoes, thinly sliced

2 medium carrots, thinly sliced

1½ cups hot water

4 teaspoons beef bouillon

1 tablespoon Worcestershire sauce

2 tablespoons oil

Butter or margarine

❖ Preheat the oven to 325°F.

Combine the flour, celery seed, salt, and pepper on a flat plate. Dredge the meat in the flour mixture, coating well. Brown the meat in oil. Layer the meat, onion, potatoes, and carrots in a large baking dish with a tight-fitting lid.

Combine the hot water and bouillon in a small bowl, and mix well; stir in the Worcestershire. Pour over the meat and vegetables. Dot the casserole with butter. Bake 3 hours.

Roasted Asparagus

Everyone looks forward to springtime, when the asparagus is in season. This recipe is nothing fancy or complicated, but it is one of those seasonal treats that we wait patiently for every year.

—†|¶—

YIELD: 4 SERVINGS

10 to 15 medium-size spears green or purple heirloom asparagus, such as Conover's colossal

¼ teaspoon sea salt

¼ teaspoon black pepper

¼ teaspoon garlic powder

½ teaspoon dried thyme, or 1 teaspoon fresh chopped thyme

1 to 2 tablespoons olive oil

1 teaspoon white wine vinegar

❖ Preheat the oven to 350°F.

Wash the asparagus, and lay in a shallow baking dish or cast-iron skillet in a single layer. Mix the salt, pepper, garlic powder, and thyme in a small bowl, and set aside. Drizzle the olive oil and vinegar over the asparagus. Sprinkle the seasoning on top of the asparagus, and bake in the oven for 20 to 25 minutes or until the asparagus is barely tender. Serve immediately.

HEIRLOOM:
CONOVER'S COLOSSAL ASPARAGUS

Conover's Colossal is an American heirloom variety developed on Long Island, New York, by Abraham Van Siclen and introduced around 1870. Widely grown in years past, it was deemed to be superior to other varieties.

Heirloom asparagus must be started from seed, as crowns are not generally available for planting. Be patient—it will take four years from sowing to that first harvest. But the wait pays off: asparagus plants remain productive for ten to twenty years or longer. Conover's Colossal is one of the best varieties for general use and for growing from seed.

ROASTED ASPARAGUS

Spring Herb Salad

This is a great way to enjoy loose-leaf lettuce such as Black-Seeded Simpson, a popular American heirloom dating back to the 1870s. It has light green crinkly leaves and a crisp, juicy taste.

YIELD: 4 TO 6 SERVINGS

1 pound mixed baby salad greens (such as leaf lettuce, spinach, arugula, mustard greens, mâche)

¼ cup chopped chives

¼ cup chopped green onions

4 ounces crumbled feta cheese

4 tablespoons sunflower seeds or chopped walnuts

HERB DRESSING

¼ cup red wine vinegar

¼ cup water

½ cup olive oil

2 teaspoons dried oregano

2 teaspoons dried basil

1 to 2 cloves garlic, crushed

½ teaspoon sea salt

¼ teaspoon Dijon mustard

¼ teaspoon freshly ground black pepper

❖ Place all dressing ingredients in a blender, and blend for 1 minute. Refrigerate in a glass jar for at least 4 hours, preferably overnight.

When the dressing is chilled, combine the greens, chives, green onions, feta cheese, and sunflower seeds or walnuts in a large bowl. Toss well with enough dressing to lightly coat the salad ingredients.

Mustard Potato Salad

This potato salad is the old favorite with a twist that makes it special. The eggs give it extra body, and the peppers and mustard add spice. Fingerling potato varieties are small, finger-size tubers with reliable flavor and quality. Most fingerlings stay firm when cooked, so any variety will perform well in this salad.

YIELD: 6 TO 8 SERVINGS

3 pounds heirloom fingerling potatoes, such as Russian Banana, peeled and boiled until tender

3 hard-cooked large eggs

1 small onion, finely chopped

1 stalk celery, finely chopped

½ red bell pepper, finely chopped

¼ cup chopped roasted red peppers

½ cup sweet pickle relish

1 cup mayonnaise

2 teaspoons prepared mustard

Salt and pepper, to taste

❖ Cut the potatoes into small cubes, and place in a medium bowl. Chop the eggs and add to the potatoes. Add onion, celery, bell pepper, roasted red peppers, and relish; mix well. Combine the mayonnaise and mustard in a small bowl, then stir into the potato mixture until well coated. Add salt and pepper to taste. Chill to meld flavors.

HEIRLOOM:
RUSSIAN BANANA FINGERLING POTATO

The Russian Banana was developed in the Baltic region of Eurasia and was introduced to British Columbia by Russian settlers, probably in the late nineteenth century. An heirloom gourmet variety and a favorite among chefs, the Russian Banana is a yellow banana-shaped firm, waxy tuber. This versatile variety of potato retains its wonderful flavor with baking, boiling, and steaming, making it an excellent choice for salads.

Wilted Spinach Salad

|||

YIELD: 4 SERVINGS

1 pound fresh heirloom spinach leaves, such as Bloomsdale
    Long Standing, stems removed and washed

¼ cup chopped green onions

2 hard-cooked eggs, peeled and chopped

1 cup chopped mushrooms

4 slices bacon

¼ cup vinegar

¼ cup water

1 tablespoon sugar

Salt and pepper, to taste

1 cup croutons

❖ Tear the spinach leaves into bite-size pieces, and place in a large bowl. Add green onions, chopped eggs, and mushrooms.

Fry the bacon in a medium skillet until crisp; drain, reserving the drippings. Crumble the bacon and place on the greens. Add vinegar, water, and sugar to the pan drippings. Cook and stir until well blended. Pour the hot dressing over the spinach, and mix well. Top with croutons and serve immediately.

HEIRLOOM:
BLOOMSDALE LONG STANDING SPINACH

Bloomsdale Long Standing spinach (named so because it stands two weeks longer than most varieties) was developed in 1925. Today, it is the most popular and readily available nonhybrid spinach, with various strains being available. It performs better in hot weather than most varieties and produces glossy, deep green savoy leaves. Bloomsdale has a rich, mild, and tender flavor, perfect for fresh eating or served wilted, as in the Wilted Spinach Salad recipe.

Easy Salad Dressing

YIELD: 2 CUPS

1 spring onion bulb

½ teaspoon sea salt

¼ teaspoon sugar

½ cup your choice vinegar (champagne, red wine, balsamic, rice wine)

1 cup extra-virgin olive oil

Coarsely ground black pepper

1 tablespoon chopped oregano or marjoram

1 tablespoon coarsely ground mustard or Dijon

❖ Mince the onion and place in a small bowl. Sprinkle with salt and sugar, and cover with vinegar. Allow the onion to stand at least 30 minutes.

In a tight-sealing jar, mix the olive oil, pepper, and oregano. Stir together the mustard, vinegar, and onions, then add to the olive oil. Place the cap on the jar, and shake well to combine. The dressing will separate as it sits, so be certain to shake vigorously before dressing the salad greens. (You may keep this dressing on hand, refrigerated, for up to a week.)

Quick Pickled Radishes

Radishes are often the first spring harvest from the garden, but they don't last long in season. Small, round, and quick-growing varieties should be harvested when they are roughly the size of olives or cherries (¾ inch in diameter). Try the mildly sweet Early Scarlet Globe radish or the mildly pungent oblong French Breakfast variety that was offered in seed catalogs as early as 1885 and is still popular today with heirloom enthusiasts.

YIELD: 4 SERVINGS

12 small radishes (about 2 cups)

4 tablespoons sugar

2 tablespoons salt

2 bay leaves

2 cloves garlic, crushed

2 tablespoons cider vinegar

1 teaspoon crushed red pepper (optional)

❖ Cut off the tops of the radishes, and score the bottoms with an X about ¼-inch deep.

Place all ingredients in a glass bowl. Cover and shake to coat the radishes. Leave covered overnight or at least 5 hours before serving.

Greens with Garlic Dressing

YIELD: 6 SERVINGS

3 cups torn heirloom spinach leaves, such as Bloomsdale
   Long Standing

2 cups torn heirloom romaine (also called cos) leaves, such
   as Rouge d'Hiver

1 cup mixed greens

1 11-ounce can mandarin oranges, drained

1 small red onion, thinly sliced

¼ cup toasted almonds

GARLIC DRESSING

5 tablespoons olive oil

2 tablespoons red wine vinegar

1 teaspoon garlic salt

1 clove garlic, crushed

⅛ teaspoon black pepper

❖ Whisk all the dressing ingredients in a small bowl. Let stand 15 minutes. Strain to remove garlic before using.

Place the salad greens in a large bowl. Top with oranges, onion, and almonds. Toss with garlic dressing. Serve immediately.

HEIRLOOM: ROUGE D'HIVER LETTUCE

Romaine, also known as cos, a heading lettuce with erect leaves, gets its name from the Romans, who popularized this type of lettuce after finding it growing on the Greek island of Cos. Rouge d'Hiver ("red winter") is a French heirloom with striking red and green coloration developed in the 1840s. It is an early variety (first crop is usually ready for harvest in March), and its upright plants can tolerate cold conditions as well as heat. Rouge d'Hiver's leaves are tender and smooth in texture with a delicious sweet flavor.

Sautéed Lettuce and Wild Mushrooms

Sautéed lettuce was served in ancient Rome when older leaves were cooked with oil and vinegar. This sauté serves as a great accompaniment to grilled meat, vegetables, or seafood because of its combination of freshness and earthiness.

YIELD: 4 SERVINGS

1 tablespoon extra-virgin olive oil

2 tablespoons butter

½ pound wild mushrooms, stems removed, wiped clean, and
    sliced

Salt and pepper, to taste

1 pound chopped heirloom Bibb lettuce, such as Limestone
    Bibb

½ cup cream

1 teaspoon fresh thyme

❖ In a medium saucepan, heat the olive oil. Add the butter, and allow it to melt. When the pan is hot and the butter is beginning to brown, add the mushrooms and let them cook for 2 to 3 minutes or until brown. Stir the mushrooms, and season with salt and pepper to taste.

Once the mushrooms are tender and most of the moisture has evaporated, add the lettuce. Season with additional salt and pepper, if needed, cooking until the lettuce is tender. Add the cream and the thyme. Cook until the cream is reduced and thickened. Remove from heat. Serve warm.

HEIRLOOM:
LIMESTONE BIBB LETTUCE

Bibb, butterhead, or Boston types, as they are generally known, are tender, floppy-headed lettuces with fine, delicate flavor. Originating in Kentucky in 1850 and named for the commonwealth's abundant limestone, Limestone Bibb was the first American gourmet lettuce. Its small, compact head has smooth, thick, dark green leaves and inner leaves of golden yellow. Limestone is crisp, with a nice creamy flavor.

Dilled Brussels Sprouts

YIELD: 8 SERVINGS

2 pounds (about 8 cups) small heirloom brussels sprouts, such as Catskill

6 tablespoons butter

2 tablespoons finely chopped onion

2 tablespoons fresh chopped dill

Salt and pepper, to taste

Toasted almonds (optional)

❖ Wash the sprouts and blot dry. Pull off loose or pale leaves and discard. Cover the brussels sprouts with salted water in a large saucepan. Cook about 10 to 15 minutes or until crisp tender, monitoring closely to avoid overcooking. Drain and cool, then cut into ¼-inch slices.

Melt the butter in a large skillet. Add the onion and sauté until tender. Stir in the dill. Add the sprouts, and cook until they are well coated with butter and dill. Season to taste.

Spoon sprouts into a serving dish. Top with toasted almonds, if desired.

SMALLER IS BETTER

Brussels sprouts seem to evoke the same response from children and adults alike—"Ick!" Brussels sprouts have been historically disliked because they have been the victim of bad cooking—overcooking, to be precise. A properly steamed sprout will produce a sweet, nutty flavor that is irresistible to any vegetable lover. For superior taste, seek out heirloom varieties of brussels sprouts such as Catskill or Long Island Improved (developed around 1890). They are smaller than the enormous hybrids common today but certainly more delicious. Select sprouts that are bright in color, firm, and no larger than 1 to 2 inches in diameter.

DILLED BRUSSELS SPROUTS

New Peas and Potatoes

Shelling peas should be harvested and shucked when the peas have swelled inside their pods.

YIELD: 6 SERVINGS

3 cups fresh heirloom shelled peas, such as Lincoln
　Homesteader

12 small new potatoes

1½ teaspoons salt

1½ cups milk

1½ teaspoons unbleached all-purpose flour

2 tablespoons butter

Salt and pepper, to taste

❖ Boil the peas and potatoes in separate saucepans in salted water until tender. Drain both pans. Add the peas to the potatoes, and pour the milk over them. Combine the flour and butter until crumbly. Heat the milk on medium high until almost boiling. Stir in the butter mixture. Cook, stirring constantly, until thickened. Season with salt and pepper to taste.

HEIRLOOM:
LINCOLN HOMESTEADER PEA

Early American homesteaders enjoyed fresh sweet peas in spring but also dried them for later use in winter soups and stews. The Lincoln variety of shelling peas, which is also known as Homesteader, was developed before 1908 and has tightly packed pods with small, wrinkled, cream-colored peas. Lincoln is still widely available today because of its unsurpassed flavor.

Coconut Cream Cheese Pound Cake

This is a delicious treat and an excellent way to use surplus eggs from your hens. Serve it with pineapple or raspberry sorbet on the side, and garnish with fresh mint leaves.

YIELD: 10 TO 12 SERVINGS

½ cup softened butter or margarine

½ cup vegetable shortening

1 8-ounce package cream cheese, softened

3 cups sugar

6 large farmstead eggs

3 cups unbleached all-purpose flour

¼ teaspoon salt

¼ teaspoon baking soda

1 6-ounce package frozen unsweetened coconut, thawed

1 teaspoon pure coconut extract

1 teaspoon pure almond extract

½ teaspoon pure vanilla extract

 Confectioners' sugar

❖ Preheat the oven to 325°F.

Grease and flour a 10-inch round tube pan.

Beat the butter, shortening, and cream cheese in a stand mixer at medium speed until creamy. Gradually add the sugar, beating 5 minutes. Crack eggs into a separate bowl, and add extracts; beat lightly. Slowly add the eggs to the sugar and butter mixture, beating just until the yolks disappear.

Combine the flour, salt, and baking soda in a small bowl, and mix well. Add to the butter mixture, mixing just until moistened through. Do not overmix. Stir in the coconut. Pour the batter into the prepared pan. Bake for 1½ hours or until a wooden skewer inserted into the center comes out clean.

Cool on a wire rack for 15 minutes. Remove from the pan, and cool completely on the wire rack. Wrap with plastic wrap. Chill if desired.

To serve, cut each piece and sift confectioners' sugar over top.

Apple of My Eye Sundae

YIELD: 2 SERVINGS

2 medium heirloom apples, such as Grimes Golden

½ cup organic apple juice or cider

¼ cup dark brown sugar, packed

½ teaspoon ground cinnamon or more, to taste

¼ teaspoon ground nutmeg or more, to taste

½ pint heavy cream

1 tablespoon pure maple syrup or maple extract

6 sugar or maple cookies, crumbled

1 pint vanilla ice cream

❖ Peel and chop the apples, and combine them with the apple cider, sugar, and spices in a large saucepan. Heat to boiling, and then reduce heat to a simmer. Stirring occasionally, simmer for 5 to 10 minutes or until apples are tender. Add more liquid if needed. Cover and set aside when done.

Combine the heavy cream and maple syrup in a chilled bowl and whip. Cover and chill in the refrigerator until needed.

In sundae glasses, layer the crumbled cookies, ice cream, and apples. Then repeat the layers until all the ingredients are used. Top with the maple-flavored whipped cream, and sprinkle with cookie crumbles. Serve with maple cookies on side.

RHUBARB PIE

Rhubarb Pie

Rhubarb can be extremely sour unless it is heavily sugared or combined with sweet fruits such as strawberries. Because this recipe doesn't use fruits, it's in special need of doctoring, so don't be shy with the sugar.

YIELD: 6 TO 8 SERVINGS

5 cups chopped heirloom rhubarb, such as Victoria, top and bottom bits cut off

1½ cups plus 1 tablespoon sugar

2 tablespoons unbleached all-purpose flour

½ teaspoon cinnamon

½ teaspoon nutmeg

2 9-inch pie shells, unbaked

Butter

1 large farmstead egg, beaten

❖ Preheat the oven to 425°F.

In a large bowl, combine rhubarb, 1½ cups sugar, flour, cinnamon, and nutmeg. Mix well, and make sure the rhubarb is well coated. Place the rhubarb mixture in one of the pie shells. Dot the top of the pie with bits of butter. Place the other pie shell over the rhubarb mixture to make a top crust. Press the edges together with your thumbs. Cut a slit in the crust to release steam. Brush with the beaten egg, and sprinkle with remaining sugar.

Bake 30 minutes or until the crust begins to brown. If the crust starts to get too dark, cover with foil for the remainder of the cooking time.

HEIRLOOM: VICTORIA RHUBARB

Rhubarb was not an accepted foodstuff until around 1809, when an Englishman named Joseph Myatt brought bundles of rhubarb to sell at market in London. The rather different astringent taste of rhubarb was not an immediate hit with the locals. The Victoria variety, also known as Myatt's Victoria, is the standard variety of rhubarb, and Myatt eventually became known as the father of rhubarb. This variety is still popular today, and its flavor is reminiscent of wine, perfect for homemade rhubarb wine.

Rhubarb Apple Crunch

YIELD: 6 SERVINGS

1 cup unbleached all-purpose flour

1 cup old-fashioned oats

1 cup packed dark brown sugar

½ teaspoon nutmeg

½ teaspoon cinnamon

½ cup cold butter or margarine

2 cups diced fresh heirloom rhubarb, such as Victoria

2 cups diced red apples

1⅓ cups sugar

2 teaspoons cornstarch

1 cup cold water

1 teaspoon pure vanilla extract

Cinnamon ice cream (optional)

❖ Preheat the oven to 350°F.

Grease an 8 × 8–inch baking pan.

In a large bowl, combine the flour with the oats, brown sugar, nutmeg, and cinnamon. Cut the butter into the dry ingredients, and use a dough blender until the mixture resembles coarse crumbs. Pat half of the crumbs into the prepared pan to make a crust. Sprinkle the rhubarb and apples over the crust.

In a heavy medium-size saucepan, combine the sugar and cornstarch. Whisk in the water until the mixture is smooth, and then bring to a boil. Cook 2 minutes or until thickened. Remove from the heat and allow to cool slightly. Add the vanilla extract and pour over the fruit mixture. Sprinkle the remaining crumbs over the top.

Bake the crunch, uncovered, for 1 hour or until lightly browned. Serve warm with ice cream, if desired.

Cheryl's Rhubarb Cake

◢◣◤

YIELD: 8 TO 10 SERVINGS

1½ cups packed light brown sugar

½ cup butter, softened

1 large farmstead egg

1 cup buttermilk

2 cups unbleached all-purpose flour

1 teaspoon baking soda

½ teaspoon salt

1 teaspoon vanilla extract

4 cups chopped heirloom rhubarb, such as Victoria

¼ cup sugar

1 tablespoon ground cinnamon

❖ Preheat the oven to 350°F.

Grease and flour a 9 x 13-inch baking pan.

Cream the brown sugar and butter in a large bowl. Beat in the egg and the buttermilk. Combine the dry ingredients in a medium bowl, and add to the butter mixture. Mix well. Fold in the vanilla and the rhubarb. Pour into the prepared pan, and spread evenly. Combine the sugar and ground cinnamon in a small bowl, and sprinkle over the cake.

Bake 25 to 35 minutes or until a wooden pick inserted in the center comes out clean.

Rhubarb Crunch

◢◣◤

YIELD: 6 SERVINGS

½ cup butter, melted

1 cup unbleached all-purpose flour

1 cup packed light brown sugar

¾ cup oats

4 cups diced heirloom rhubarb, such as Victoria

1 cup sugar

2 tablespoons cornstarch

1 cup water

½ teaspoon vanilla extract

½ teaspoon lemon extract

1 cup fresh sliced strawberries (optional)

Vanilla ice cream (optional)

❖ Preheat the oven to 350°F.

Combine the melted butter, flour, brown sugar, and oats in a medium bowl, and mix until crumbly. Place half the mixture in an 8 x 8-inch baking dish. Top with the rhubarb.

In a saucepan, combine the sugar, cornstarch, water, vanilla extract, and lemon extract. Cook over medium heat, stirring constantly, until thick and clear. Spoon the sauce over the rhubarb. If desired, add sliced strawberries for extra sweetness. Sprinkle the remaining flour mixture on top.

Bake 1 hour, then remove to a cooling rack. Serve with vanilla ice cream, if desired.

Lime Butter Cookies

—❙❙❙—

YIELD: APPROXIMATELY 3 DOZEN COOKIES

1 cup butter

2¼ cups flour

¾ cup sugar

1½ teaspoons finely grated lime peel

2 tablespoons freshly squeezed lime juice, strained to remove pulp and seeds

1 teaspoon vanilla extract

TOPPING

2 tablespoons lime juice

¼ cup sugar

½ cup confectioners' sugar, sifted

❖Preheat the oven to 325°F.

Beat butter on medium high for 30 seconds. Add sugar, lime zest, lime juice, vanilla, and half the flour, beating until thoroughly combined. Beat in remaining flour.

Roll into 1-inch balls, and place on ungreased cookie sheet. Bake for 20 to 22 minutes or until bottoms are lightly browned. Remove from baking sheet immediately, and cool on wire racks.

TOPPING

Stir together the lime juice and sugar until the sugar is dissolved. Wait for the cookies to cool, then brush the mixture on them. Let sit for 10 minutes, then sift confectioners' sugar over tops.

LIME BUTTER COOKIES

SUMMER

 Despite all the labor-saving equipment on the market today, summer on the farm is still exhausting under its crush of constant activity. The fruits of our labor are upon us, and the flurry of outdoor activities includes harvesting crops, reseeding, weeding, watering, monitoring for pests and crop damage, making hay, and, for some, going to market. In many places, summer is marked by hot, humid days and mild evenings aglow with fireflies and the ever-present hum of cicadas and toads—music to the ears.

The hobby-farm kitchen is never busier than it is in the summer. It's alive with the sights and scents of the season: those beguiling heirloom tomatoes in every color of the rainbow, aromatic melons, and an overabundance of zucchini squash, which awaits its fate on the grill or shredded in a sweet or savory quick bread. Preserving the harvest for future months takes priority as canning and freezing become weekly—sometimes daily—chores.

THE STUFFLEBEAM FAMILY

HEIRLOOM GROWER   HOMEsweetFARM

For more than ten years, collecting and growing heirloom vegetables and herbs have been an obsession for Brad Stufflebeam. As an organic horticulture professional for fifteen years and a certified "plant nut," Brad, with his wife, Jenny, farm the twenty-two-acre HOMEsweetFARM in Washington County, the "Birthplace of Texas."

Early settlers established family farms, ranches, and dairies in Washington County, where the soil is rich and the rolling hills get dressed beautifully each spring in Texas bluebonnet. In fact, HOMEsweetFARM is located just off the well-toured Bluebonnet Trail and is lush with farkleberry shrubs (Texas native blueberry), mayhaw trees, muscadine grapes, native persimmons, oaks, pecan trees, and yaupons. Surrounded by such native abundance, the Stufflebeams have also carved out their own piece of history on this land.

They started a small specialty retail nursery in the early 1990s, and by 2002 their work had evolved into a full-time farm operation. Today, the Stufflebeams have more than six acres planted in vegetables, herbs, and flowers to supply their farm stand and their CSA business of more than sixty-five members. Their plans are to expand to twelve acres.

Among their crops are 150 varieties of open-pollinated, or heirloom, vegetables and herbs, including Banana Legs tomatoes, Beck's Big Okra, Dr. Carolyn White cherry tomatoes, Orangeglo watermelon, Pasilla Bajio chilies, Red Noodle beans, Serpent cucumbers, Tiger melon, and White Habanero chilies. In an effort to share their enthusiasm for heirloom crops with the public, the Stufflebeams host quarterly festivals on their farm. At the Tomato Festival in June, they exhibit more than thirty-five varieties of heirlooms. The Melon Fest each July showcases twenty-plus heirloom varieties. The Stufflebeams want to create a local food network that will provide seasonal food to the community, so they invite other local farmers, ranchers, and chefs to participate in the festivals and showcase their own local-food specialties.

Brad and Jenny believe that raising heritage animals is also an important aspect of their farm, as important as raising heirloom vegetables. They raise pastured chickens and offer their eggs as a value-added CSA product. The endangered Buff goose (the only domesticated goose developed in the United States); the Buff Orpington duck; and the Hamburg, the Rhode Island Red, the Welsummer, and the Wyandotte chickens are among their flock.

The Stufflebeams also keep Alpine dairy goats to supply the family's milk. "We work as a family full time on the farm," says Jenny, who also home-schools their two daughters, viewing the farm as a major educational opportunity. When not tending to the fields, Brad offers on-site consultation to others running small farms, helping them develop their land using organic and sustainable techniques. He also serves as president of the Texas Organic Farmers & Gardeners Association.

"We cook with whole foods as a way of life and make our farm's products a part of every meal," explains Jenny. "We try to discipline ourselves not to buy what we can grow and to always eat in season." The Stufflebeams's culinary independence inspires them to frequently explore ethnic cuisines such as Asian, Caribbean, and Mexican. Finding that the season controls their menu, Brad and Jenny always try to prepare new recipes so as not to fall into a rut. As a result, Jenny says, "Our children have really learned to eat most anything, and they find so much joy in eating things grown on our farm."

HOMEsweetFARM
7800 FM 2502
Brenham, TX 77833
(979) 251-9922
http://www.homesweetfarm.com

Fresh Multicolored Salsa

This salsa is easy to make with your abundance of heirloom tomatoes, fresh from the garden. Make multiple batches and freeze some for later use. Served with crunchy yellow corn tortilla chips, it's almost a meal in itself.

YIELD: 3 CUPS

8 small green heirloom tomatoes, such as Green Sausage, finely chopped

4 orange or yellow medium tomatoes, finely chopped

2 large cloves garlic, minced

½ cup diced green onions

2 to 3 jalapeños with seeds and membranes removed, minced

½ cup chopped cilantro

3 tablespoons fresh lime juice

½ teaspoon sea salt

½ teaspoon ground cumin

❖ Combine all the ingredients in a medium bowl. Let the flavors meld for at least 30 minutes before serving. Serve with tortilla chips for an appetizer or as a relish for tacos and omelets.

RAINBOW COLORS

Green heirloom tomatoes offer a spicy, sometimes tart, flavor. Varieties of green tomatoes include Green Sausage, Green Zebra, and the rare Green Grape. Yellow varieties tend to be sweet but mild and include Hugh's, Lillian's Yellow, and Manyel. Orange heirlooms are sweet and less acidic with varieties such as the popular Kellogg's Breakfast, Orange Strawberry, and Earl of Edgecombe. Countless other varieties of all colors are available through heirloom seed sources (see Appendix A). This combination of colors and flavors creates an unexpected but delightful alternative to standard red salsa.

Spinach-Mushroom Quiche

This delicious quiche makes a nice brunch offering, or you can cut it into thin wedges for an appetizer. You can also wrap individual servings and take them to a picnic.

‖

YIELD: 16 TO 18 APPETIZERS

2 9-inch deep-dish piecrusts, thawed

1 small onion, chopped

½ pound sliced fresh mushrooms

2 tablespoons olive oil

6 large farmstead eggs, beaten

½ cup half-and-half

1 8-ounce container sour cream

1 teaspoon salt

½ teaspoon black pepper

2 cups packed chopped fresh heirloom spinach, such as King of Denmark

¼ pound shredded smoked mozzarella cheese

❖ Preheat the oven to 425°F.

Prick the sides and bottom of the crusts with a fork. Bake crusts for 6 to 8 minutes. Remove from the oven, and set aside on a wire rack to cool. Reduce the oven temperature to 325°F.

Sauté the onion and mushrooms in the olive oil in a medium skillet until tender. Set aside to cool.

Combine the eggs, half-and-half, sour cream, salt, and pepper in a medium bowl. Fold in the spinach, cheese, and mushrooms. Pour the mixture into the prepared piecrusts.

Bake for 40 to 45 minutes or until a wooden pick inserted in the center of the pie comes out clean. You may need to cover the edges of crust with foil partway through the baking process to prevent overbrowning.

Let stand for 10 minutes before slicing.

Cheesy Corn Toasts

Use sweet corn fresh from your garden. The blend of sweetness from the corn, tartness from the goat cheese, and crunchiness from the toast combine for a perfect summer treat.

YIELD: 8 APPETIZERS

2 cups (about 2 ears) fresh heirloom corn, such as Golden Bantam

2 tablespoons butter

Salt and cracked pepper, to taste

½ cup cream

1 cup fresh goat cheese

2 tablespoons olive oil

8 slices French bread

❖ In a small skillet, sauté the corn in the butter with a little salt and pepper for about 15 minutes or until the corn is sweet and tender. Add the cream, and cook until the liquid is reduced by half. Cool the mixture, and puree in a food processor. Thin the pureed corn with milk if needed.

Preheat the oven to 425°F.

Add the goat cheese to the puree, and mix into a thick paste. Brush the oil onto both sides of the bread slices, and bake about 10 minutes or until golden brown. Remove the toast, and spread each slice with 2 tablespoons of the paste. Return to the oven and bake until golden brown.

HEIRLOOM:
GOLDEN BANTAM CORN

Sweet corn first appeared in American seed catalogs in 1828 as generic "sweet" or "sugar" corn, but it took many years for the taste to catch on with consumers. Sweet, white-kernel corn then became the standard, with yellow corn being considered horse corn, or livestock feed, by Americans. The Golden Bantam variety, introduced in 1902 by W. Atlee Burpee, was the first to sway public opinion. The farmer who discovered Golden Bantam in western Massachusetts, E. L. Coy, sent the seed to Burpee with a note that read, "You now own the very sweetest and richest corn ever known." Golden Bantam remains the standard for open-pollinated yellow sweet corn.

Roasted Corn, Tomato, and Black Bean Salsa

This salsa is best in summer, when all these vegetables and herbs are in season. The amount of vegetables can be widely adjusted to your personal taste in spiciness.

YIELD: SERVES 8 TO 10

2 to 3 ears white or yellow heirloom sweet corn, such as Golden Bantam

2 pounds heirloom tomatoes (use a variety of paste and slicing types)

1 large onion

1 jalapeño, Black Czech or other hot pepper

1 large sweet bell pepper

2 to 3 cloves garlic

1 29-ounce can organic black beans, rinsed and drained

⅓ cup chopped fresh cilantro

1 teaspoon sea salt

½ teaspoon ground black pepper

❖ Preheat a gas or charcoal grill.

Pull back the husks from the corn, and remove the silk. Pull the husks back over the kernels, and soak the corn in water for several minutes. Roast the corn on the grill for about 10 to 15 minutes on the top rack, turning constantly. Remove from the heat, cool, and remove the husks. Remove the corn from the cob using a sharp paring knife, and set aside.

Roast the tomatoes on the top rack of the grill until they are just tender and skins are charred. Remove from the grill, and let cool. Remove the skins, and set aside. Roast the onion, jalapeño pepper, and bell pepper on the grill until tender; cool slightly. Place the tomatoes, onion, jalapeño pepper, bell pepper, and garlic in a food processor. Pulse until chopped and blended. Pour into a medium bowl; add the corn and black beans, and mix well. Stir in the cilantro, salt, and pepper.

Refrigerate for 1 hour to allow the flavors to mix. Enjoy with your favorite corn tortilla chips or as part of any Mexican meal.

Cream of Tomato and Basil Soup

YIELD: 6 TO 8 SERVINGS

2 tablespoons olive oil

1/3 cup finely chopped shallots

3 cloves garlic, minced

2 10 ½-ounce cans condensed chicken broth, fat removed

3 cups chopped red heirloom tomatoes

1 apple, peeled, cored, and diced

Freshly ground black pepper

1½ cups heavy cream

¼ cup finely chopped fresh basil

❖ In a heavy 3- or 4-quart saucepan, heat the olive oil over medium-high heat. Add the shallots and garlic,

and sauté over medium heat until softened but not brown. Stir in the chicken broth, tomatoes, and apple. Add the black pepper to taste. Bring to a boil, reduce heat, and simmer uncovered for 10 minutes.

Fold the cream into the tomato mixture. Bring just to a boil, immediately reduce heat, and simmer gently for 5 minutes. Add the fresh basil. Serve immediately.

If a creamier soup is desired, before adding the cream and basil, blend the mixture in a blender (2 cups at a time), and return to the saucepan. Then fold in the cream and heat until warm. Stir in the basil before serving.

TOMATO AND ZUCCHINI CROSTINI WITH CANADIAN BACON

Tomato and Zucchini Crostini with Canadian Bacon

YIELD: 18 TO 20 SERVINGS

1½ cups chopped fresh heirloom tomatoes, seeds removed

½ cup finely chopped zucchini, such as Cocozelle

½ cup finely chopped yellow summer squash

3 tablespoons minced shallots

3 tablespoons chopped fresh basil

Salt and freshly ground black pepper, to taste

2 tablespoons olive oil

2 teaspoons minced garlic

½ cup diced Canadian bacon

One loaf baguette-style French bread, cut into ½-inch
   diagonal slices

Olive oil

❖ Preheat the oven to broil, adjusting the rack so it is 4 to 6 inches from the heat.

Combine the tomatoes, zucchini, summer squash, shallots, basil, and salt and pepper in a medium bowl. Set aside.

Heat the 2 tablespoons of olive oil in a small heavy-bottom saucepan over medium-high heat. Add the garlic and Canadian bacon, and sauté until the bacon is heated through, about 1 to 2 minutes. Do not let the garlic get too brown. Remove from the heat, and stir into the tomato mixture.

Place the bread slices on an ungreased baking sheet. Using a pastry brush, lightly brush tops with olive oil. Broil the bread for 30 to 45 seconds or until lightly toasted. Top each slice with 1 to 2 tablespoons of the vegetable-bacon mixture. Serve immediately.

HEIRLOOM: COCOZELLE SQUASH

Cocozelle originated in Italy in the 1800s as Cocozella di Napoli and was introduced in the United States in 1934. This zucchini squash grows as a bush and produces distinctive dark and light green-striped fruits with firm, tender flesh and a nutty flavor. Fruits taste best when picked very small but remain tasty up to 12 inches in length.

Gazpacho

This zesty chilled soup is a delicious way to get your vitamins. Packed with nutrients and brimming with flavor, it makes a refreshing snack, an elegant first course, or when fortified with your favorite beans and feta cheese, a light meal. Experiment with any heirloom-variety tomatoes for classic true tomato flavor.

YIELD: 10 TO 12 SERVINGS

8 medium heirloom tomatoes, cored and coarsely chopped

1 clove garlic, minced

4 tablespoons lemon juice

½ cup chopped parsley

5 cups tomato juice

½ cup olive oil

1 tablespoon chili garlic sauce

2 green bell peppers, finely chopped

2 large white heirloom onions, such as White Portugal, finely chopped

2 large heirloom cucumbers, such as Suyo Long, peeled, seeded, and diced

Salt and pepper, to taste

Chopped parsley for garnish (optional)

Garlic croutons

GARLIC CROUTONS

2 large cloves garlic, minced

¼ cup olive oil

½ loaf French bread, cut into 1-inch cubes

❖ Working in two batches, combine the first seven ingredients in a blender. Puree until smooth. Pour into a large bowl, and add the green pepper, onion, and cucumber. Stir until combined, seasoning with salt and pepper to taste. Chill thoroughly.

Top individual bowls with garlic croutons and chopped parsley, if desired.

GARLIC CROUTONS

If it's too hot to heat up the oven for these, use packaged croutons or crumble rye crackers on top of the soup.

Preheat the oven to 350°F. Simmer the garlic in olive oil over very low heat until soft. Strain the oil from the garlic using a fine-mesh strainer. With the bowl of a spoon, mash cooked garlic into the oil. Place bread cubes on a large baking sheet, and brush with garlic oil. Toast for 30 minutes or until crisp and golden, stirring every 10 minutes.

Roasted Purple Peppers

Serve this colorful dish as part of an antipasto plate or with bread and fresh mozzarella as a first course.

YIELD: 8 TO 10 SERVINGS

8 purple peppers, such as Purple Beauty

1 cup extra-virgin olive oil

Sea salt and coarsely ground black pepper, to taste

¼ cup white balsamic vinegar

HEIRLOOM: PURPLE BEAUTY PEPPER

The Purple Beauty sweet pepper is not necessarily an heirloom, but it does qualify as rare. Developed through the dehybridization* of the Purple Belle variety, this beautiful purple bell pepper produces blocky 3 × 3–inch fruits that begin ripening as an emerald green and mature to a stunning deep eggplant purple. Some people consider Purple Beauty to be the best open-pollinated purple bell pepper on the seed market. With thick, meaty walls, a tender-crisp texture, and a mild-sweet flavor, this pepper is ideal for slicing, for stir frying, or for adding color to salads.

* Dehybridization is the time-consuming process of growing, selecting seed, and growing for successive generations to create an open-pollinated variety from a known hybrid.

❖ Preheat the oven to broiler setting on high.

In a large bowl, toss the whole peppers with enough olive oil to coat; salt and pepper to taste. Line the peppers on a baking sheet. Place the baking sheet as close to the broiler as possible, and broil 5 to 6 minutes or until skin is burnt and cracking. Remove the peppers from the oven, and flip them over. Return the peppers to the oven, and allow the opposite side to burn and crack. Repeat until the entire surface of the pepper is charred. Place all the peppers back into the bowl, and cover tightly with plastic wrap.

Allow the peppers to sit until cool to the touch. At this point, the skin should be loose and easily removed. Remove as much skin as possible, but do not rinse with water. Once the skin is removed, open the peppers to remove the seeds. Cut the peppers into strips, as long and thin as you like. Place the strips in a clean bowl, and toss with the white balsamic vinegar and remaining olive oil.

Refrigerate for at least 2 hours before serving.

Watermelon and Mint Aguas Frescas

When we think watermelon, we usually think of simply savoring it fresh, sliced, and chilled. But watermelon is more versatile than that. It can be made into refreshing sorbet; incorporated in a tangy, syrupy fruit salad; and blended into a tasty beverage for serving at a summer cookout. This recipe is a take on the Mexican drinks that can be found almost anywhere in Mexico and are also popular in the Southwest United States.

YIELD: 4 SERVINGS

5 cups heirloom watermelon chunks, such as Moon and Stars, seeds removed and chilled in the freezer for several hours

¼ cup mint leaves

1 cup water

4 mint sprigs

❖ In a blender, combine the watermelon, mint leaves, and water until smooth. To transport to a picnic, pour into a well-chilled thermos. Serve in tall glasses with a mint sprig for garnish.

HEIRLOOM: MOON AND STARS WATERMELON

The legendary heirloom Moon and Stars watermelon seed was thought for a long time to have been permanently lost. Rediscovered growing in Missouri in the 1980s by Seed Savers Exchange's Kent Whealy, this variety has enjoyed a tremendous resurgence ever since. Moon and Stars is so named for its speckled yellow spots, several small ones (stars), and at least one rather large one (moon) set against its dark green skin. Fruits are medium large (25 to 30 pounds or more). This is one of the sweetest of all watermelons.

SUMMER CORN CHOWDER

Summer Corn Chowder

This is a nice soup to have during the sweet-corn season, or it can be made with stored vegetables in winter. Use Golden Bantam or Country Gentleman, both of which provide a good crunchy and "corny" taste. (However, note that heirloom sweet corn is not as sweet as modern supersweet varieties.) The fresh corn and parsley used in summer will give this soup a fresh taste that you just can't duplicate in winter.

YIELD: 6 TO 8 SERVINGS

4 to 6 thick bacon slices, chopped into ½-inch pieces

1 large red or white onion, chopped

3 cups water

3 cups heirloom potatoes, such as Bintje, Garnet Chili, or
    Lady Finger, cut into small chunks

2 cloves garlic, crushed

3 tablespoons butter

¼ cup unbleached all-purpose flour

2 cups milk

1 teaspoon sea salt

¼ teaspoon black pepper

1 cup diced or chopped ham

4 to 6 ears fresh heirloom sweet corn, cut from cob

1 tablespoon chopped fresh parsley

❖ In a large dutch oven, cook the bacon until crisp. Remove the bacon and cook the onion in the bacon drippings until soft but not browned. Remove the onion, and drain the dutch oven.

Combine the water, potatoes, and garlic in the dutch oven. Cook until the potatoes are tender, 15 to 20 minutes. Remove the potato and garlic mixture, including any liquid, and set aside.

Melt butter in the dutch oven, and add the flour. Cook until bubbly. Add milk and cook on medium heat, stirring often until the smooth white sauce thickens. Add the potato mixture, and season with salt and pepper. Stir in the ham, corn, parsley, bacon, and onion. Heat until almost boiling (but do not boil it).

Serve warm with garlic toast and a mixed salad.

Blueberry Buttermilk Pancakes

YIELD: 4 TO 6 SERVINGS

1 cup unbleached all-purpose flour

½ teaspoon baking soda

½ teaspoon salt

2½ teaspoons baking powder

1 tablespoon cinnamon

3 large farmstead eggs, separated

1 cup sour cream

1 cup buttermilk

4 tablespoons butter, melted

1 cup fresh blueberries

❖ Stir the flour, baking soda, salt, baking powder, cinnamon, egg yolks, sour cream, and buttermilk together in a large bowl. Add the melted butter, and stir well.

Beat the egg whites in a medium bowl until stiff. Fold the whites into the flour mixture, then gradually add the blueberries.

Using a ¼-cup measuring cup, drop the batter onto a hot greased griddle. Flip when the surface is covered with bubbles, and cook until browned.

Serve with pure maple or blueberry syrup.

BLUEBERRIES

Blueberries are one of three fruits native to North America (the others being cranberries and Concord grapes). Native Americans used the berries, leaves, and roots for medicinal purposes, and early settlers prized the berries for use as a fabric dye and as a foodstuff. People incorporated blueberries into soups, stews, and dried jerky, and they ate them fresh off the bush.

The most popular cultivated variety of blueberry is *Vaccinium corymbosum,* known as the highbush blueberry (wild varieties are known as lowbush). In the early 1900s, the wild blueberry plant was domesticated through the breeding efforts of Elizabeth White and Dr. Frederick Coville, and the modern cultivated blueberry industry was born. Their work

resulted in the consistent, plump, and sweet cultivated highbush blueberries we enjoy today.

North America is the world's leading blueberry producer, accounting for nearly 90 percent of world production. The North American harvest runs from mid-April through early October, with

peak harvest in July. The leading commercial blueberry variety is Bluecrop, which produces high yields of large, bright blue berries. One newer variety is Darrow, a late-midseason variety that produces large berries and that is known for its exceptional flavor.

Blueberries can be grown in the home garden as they require little space, but they are not very common because of the plant's need for highly acidic soil. Home growers must establish and maintain acidic soil over the life of the plant. Blueberry plants will bear a first crop of fruit in their third season, but they are not fully productive for about six years. Once the plant is in production, its fruit will need to be protected from birds either by using netting, noise devices, or scarecrows.

BLUEBERRY BUTTERMILK PANCAKES

Oven French Toast with Cherry Sauce

YIELD: 4 SERVINGS

½ loaf crusty French bread

3 large farmstead eggs

¾ cup heavy cream

Pinch of salt

Dash of nutmeg

½ teaspoon vanilla extract

2 tablespoons vegetable oil

2 cups pitted and halved cherries

1 10-ounce jar cherry preserves

❖ Preheat the oven to 400°F.

Slice the bread into eight ½-inch slices. Whisk the eggs in a large bowl until fluffy. Add the cream, salt, nutmeg, and vanilla and blend well. Soak the bread, a few slices at a time, in the egg mixture.

Heat a large skillet or griddle. Add the oil. Brown the soaked bread on both sides, remove from the pan, and place on paper towels to drain. Then place on a baking sheet. Bake the bread 5 to 8 minutes to allow it to puff up.

Combine the cherries and cherry preserves in a small saucepan and heat well. Serve the French toast with butter and the cherry sauce.

Summer Berry Scones

¶¶¶

YIELD: 12 SCONES

4 cups unbleached all-purpose flour

1 tablespoon baking powder

1 teaspoon baking soda

½ teaspoon salt

⅔ cup sugar

2½ sticks cold unsalted butter, cut into 1/4-inch cubes

2 large farmstead eggs

¾ cup cold buttermilk

1½ teaspoons vanilla extract

1½ teaspoons almond extract

1 tablespoon raspberry preserves

½ cup dried currants

¾ cup blueberries, rinsed and dried on paper towels

⅔ cup raspberries, rinsed and dried on paper towels

❖ Position the rack in the center of the oven. Preheat the oven to 400°F. Line a baking sheet with parchment paper.

Place the dry ingredients in the bowl of a food processor fitted with a metal blade. Pulse to mix. Add the butter to the bowl, and run the processor for 15 seconds. Switch to pulse, and continue to pulse until no chunks of butter are left and the mixture looks grainy, like moist crumbs. Remove the blade, and spoon the crumbs into a large bowl.

Whisk the eggs in a small bowl. Whisk in the buttermilk and extracts. Whisk in the preserves and currants. Pour the wet ingredients over the dry ingredients. Mix with a wooden spoon until only a small amount of flour is visible. Add the berries and stir gently, being careful not to mash them.

Using a ½-cup measuring cup, scoop the batter and place on baking sheet, leaving 2 inches between scones. Bake 20 to 25 minutes or until the tops are golden brown and a toothpick inserted in center comes out clean. Remove from the oven, and place on a wire rack to cool slightly.

Serve warm or at room temperature with butter and jam.

Blueberry Coffee Cake

¶¶¶

YIELD: 6 TO 8 SERVINGS

¼ cup shortening

¾ cup plus ½ cup sugar

1 large farmstead egg, beaten

½ teaspoon almond extract

2 cups plus ⅓ cup unbleached all-purpose flour

2 teaspoons baking powder

½ teaspoon salt

½ cup buttermilk

2 cups blueberries

½ teaspoon cinnamon

¼ cup butter

❖ Preheat the oven to 375°F.

Grease and flour a 9 x 13–inch baking pan.

Cream the shortening and the ¾ cup sugar in a large bowl. Add the egg and mix well. Add the almond extract. Sift the 2 cups flour, baking powder, and salt in a medium bowl. Add to the creamed mixture alternately with the buttermilk. Pour the batter into the prepared pan. Sprinkle with the blueberries.

Combine the remaining ½ cup sugar, ⅓ cup flour, cinnamon, and butter in a small bowl, mixing until crumbly. Sprinkle over the blueberries, and bake 45 to 50 minutes.

Warm and Peachy Breakfast Casserole

YIELD: 6 TO 8 SERVINGS

3 medium-size freestone peaches, peeled and sliced into
¼-inch pieces

1 tablespoon brown sugar and 1 tablespoon white sugar for
tossing

1 8¾-ounce can crushed pineapple, undrained

⅓ cup fresh blueberries

1 spice cake mix

1 stick cold butter or margarine

½ cup chopped pecans

Unsweetened shredded coconut

PEELING PEACHES

To easily peel a peach, score an *X* on the bottom, place
the peach in a strainer, and dip it into boiling water for
30 to 60 seconds. Immediately plunge it into cold water
to cool. The skin will easily peel off with a sharp paring
knife.

❖ Preheat the oven to 350°F.

Place the peaches in a glass bowl. Toss with the brown
and white sugars. Spread the peaches on the bottom
of a 9 × 13–inch glass baking dish. Spread the crushed
pineapple on top. Add the blueberries. Sprinkle cake
mix evenly on top of the fruit. Cut the butter into
chunks, and spread over the cake mix. Sprinkle with
nuts and coconut.

Bake uncovered for 30 minutes. Top with foil and continue to bake for 40 minutes. Uncover and serve warm
with whipped cream.

PEACHES

Peaches originated in China more than 3,000 years ago. They arrived in the New World on the ships of Spanish explorers. Several Native American tribes cultivated peaches and are thought to be responsible for the spread of the fruit in North America.

In the early 1800s, Thomas Jefferson planted as many as thirty-eight varieties of peaches at Monticello—noteworthy because very few cultivars were available at that time. Heath Cling, Oldmixon Cling, and Morris' Red Rareripe were the first American peach varieties cultivated by Jefferson. Peaches were a popular crop for

colonists because they were easy to grow, the trees bore fruit quickly (two or three seasons after plant-ing), and the peaches were easily propagated from seed.

Peaches are classified into two categories: freestone and cling-stone. With freestone varieties, the flesh easily separates from the pit, whereas the clingstone varieties leave some flesh attached to the center stone. Clingstone's popular-ity has diminished in recent years, with the freestone and semifree-stone (combination of freestone and clingstone) becoming the peaches of choice with consumers. Freestone varieties include Red-top, Elegant Lady, and O'Henry; a semifreestone variety is Crest. Clingstone varieties are rarely sold in the markets but used in processed peach products.

Italian Zucchini Crescent Pie

YIELD: 6 SERVINGS

4 cups thinly sliced heirloom zucchini, such as Cocozelle or Black Zucchini

1 cup chopped onion

2 tablespoons butter or margarine

½ cup chopped fresh parsley or 2 tablespoons dried parsley flakes

½ teaspoon salt

½ teaspoon black pepper

½ teaspoon garlic powder

2 tablespoons chopped fresh basil or ¼ teaspoon chopped dried basil

2 tablespoons chopped fresh oregano or ¼ teaspoon chopped dried oregano

2 large farmstead eggs, beaten

2 cups shredded mozzarella or Muenster cheese

1 8-ounce can refrigerated quick crescent-shaped dinner rolls

2 teaspoons mustard

❖ Combine the zucchini, onion, and butter in a medium skillet over medium-high heat. Cook 10 minutes, stirring constantly. Remove from heat and add parsley, salt, pepper, garlic powder, basil, and oregano. Mix well. Combine the eggs and cheese in a small bowl. Stir into the zucchini mixture.

Preheat the oven to 375°F.

Separate the rolls into eight triangles. Press over the bottom and sides of an ungreased 10-inch pie pan to form a crust. Spread the mustard on the crust. Pour the vegetable mixture into the crust.

Bake about 8 minutes or until the center is set. Cover the crust with foil, and bake 10 minutes longer. Place pie on a wire rack and let cool 10 minutes before serving.

SUMMER SQUASH

Cucurbita pepo includes all of the standard summer squashes such as zucchini, pattypan (or scallop), and summer crookneck, which are eaten in their fresh, tender state. Summer squash grows like gangbusters, so it must be watched daily for harvestable fruit. Keep it well picked to encourage continuous production. Zucchini tastes best when it is 4 to 8 inches long, but it can remain tasty even when quite large. Overmature, enormous squash can be stuffed and baked or grated and used in quick-bread recipes. Heirloom varieties include Black Zucchini, introduced in 1931, and Cocozelle, a classic Italian heirloom introduced in 1934 (see page 79).

Roasted Tomato and Garlic Sauce

🍴

YIELD: 6 SERVINGS

2 to 3 pounds ripe heirloom paste tomatoes, such as Amish Paste

1 bulb garlic, with cloves separated

2 sprigs fresh oregano

4 to 6 leaves fresh basil

2 tablespoons extra-virgin olive oil

½ teaspoon sea salt

¼ teaspoon freshly ground black pepper

❖ Preheat the oven to 375°F.

Wash and core the tomatoes. Place the tomatoes evenly in a shallow 9 x 9–inch baking pan. Add the garlic cloves, tucking them in by the tomatoes. Tuck the oregano sprigs and the basil leaves in between the tomatoes and the garlic. Drizzle the olive oil over the top, and then sprinkle with salt and pepper.

Place the pan on the middle rack of the oven, and bake for 45 minutes to 1 hour or until the tomatoes are slightly blackened on top, the skins come off easily, and the juice around the tomatoes is bubbling. Remove from the oven, and cool enough to handle safely.

Run the tomatoes, garlic, and herbs all together through a food mill with a medium screen to remove tomato skins and garlic husks. If you do not have a food mill, use a colander over a pan and squish out the tomato sauce using a heavy wooden spoon. The thick, aromatic sauce is now ready to use for pasta or meat.

SANDWICHES WITH CHERRY CHUTNEY

Sandwiches with Cherry Chutney

CHERRY CHUTNEY

1 pound pitted and coarsely chopped dark sweet cherries

1 cup packed light brown sugar

1 cup peeled and finely chopped tart green apple, such as Newtown Pippin

½ cup finely chopped sweet white onion

⅓ cup cider vinegar

1 teaspoon dry mustard

1 teaspoon cinnamon

½ teaspoon powdered ginger

¼ teaspoon cloves

¼ teaspoon allspice

Dash of cayenne pepper

❖ Combine all the ingredients in a 3-quart saucepan. Bring to a boil over high heat, stirring frequently. Reduce the heat to medium low, and boil gently until the mixture is thick, about 50 to 60 minutes. Stir occasionally, increasing the frequency toward the end of the cooking process to avoid burning. Cool before serving, and store leftovers in the refrigerator.

SANDWICHES

Try one of these combinations with cherry chutney:

- Smoked turkey, spinach, and Swiss cheese on a kaiser roll

- Roast pork, leaf lettuce, and Edam or Gouda cheese on country rye bread

- Grilled chicken breast, romaine lettuce, and Havarti cheese on sourdough bread or roll

To assemble, spread mayonnaise (if desired) on bottom halves of bread or roll, then layer the greens, cheese, and meat. Top with 2 tablespoons of cherry chutney. Cover with the top halves of the bread or roll.

Fresh Heirloom Tomato Pizza

YIELD: 6 TO 8 SERVINGS

1 prepared pizza crust

2 to 3 tablespoons olive oil, divided

1 teaspoon minced garlic

Black pepper, to taste

1 pound boneless, skinless chicken breast

¼ cup minced fresh basil

1 teaspoon minced fresh oregano

2 to 3 multicolored heirloom tomatoes

¼ medium-size red onion

½ medium-size red, green, purple, orange, or yellow bell pepper

1 pound mozzarella or provolone cheese, shredded

¼ to ½ cup grated parmigiano-reggiano cheese

❖ Place the crust on a pizza pan or baking sheet.

Combine 1 tablespoon olive oil and the garlic in a small bowl. Add pepper to taste. Let stand for a few minutes.

Heat the remaining olive oil in a small skillet. Cut the chicken breast into ½- to 1-inch pieces, and place in the skillet. Cook until the chicken begins to turn white, then add the basil and oregano and continue cooking 10 to 15 minutes or until the chicken is cooked through.

Brush the olive oil and garlic mixture on the pizza crust with a pastry brush. Slice the tomatoes and place on top of the oiled crust. Sprinkle with a little basil, if desired. Add onion and pepper. Add the cooked chicken, and cover with the cheeses.

Bake according to pizza crust package instructions (usually 15 to 20 minutes at 375°F to 400°F).

HEIRLOOM: HEIRLOOM TOMATOES

Tomatoes rank as America's number one home-garden crop year after year. They are prized by seed savers and heirloom zealots, and they continually captivate home gardeners. No fruit has the favorable notoriety attained by the tasty, juicy heirloom tomato. Why? In contrast to the pale, bland, and insipid hybrids found in the supermarket, heirloom tomatoes exist in a wild array of shapes and colors, and their earthy flavors range from spicy to sweet to tangy. In addition, their enchant-ing histories are detailed in books dedicated to the subject. With names such as Boxcar Willie, Cherokee Chocolate, Jefferson Giant, Mortgage Lifter, Orange Strawberry, and Plum Lemon, among countless others, it's not difficult to imagine the rainbow of sizes, shapes, colors, and flavors present in heirloom-variety toma-toes. Such tomatoes are guilty of enticing even the most timid gar-deners into experimenting with heirlooms simply because they are so exciting.

FRESH HEIRLOOM TOMATO PIZZA

Linguine with Fresh Marinara Sauce

Paste tomatoes work well for making sauces because of their dry flesh and few seeds. Heirloom paste varieties include Long Tom, Martino's Roma, Amish Paste, and Opalka. This recipe is a great way to process the overabundance of fresh tomatoes from your garden in late August and September. Freeze each batch individually in plastic containers. When ready to use, defrost in the microwave, pour into a saucepan, add 1 tablespoon olive oil, and heat for 15 minutes to reduce the liquid. The earthy taste and smell will jolt you back to summer, even in the dead of winter.

YIELD: 4 SERVINGS

3½ cups finely chopped red heirloom paste tomatoes

2 tablespoons extra-virgin olive oil

1 medium onion, chopped

4 cloves garlic, crushed

1 cup chopped fresh basil

½ cup red wine

1 tablespoon sugar

1 tablespoon lemon juice

Salt and freshly ground pepper, to taste

1 pound linguine

Freshly grated Parmesan cheese (optional)

❖ Blanch the whole tomatoes until skins are loose. Cool in cold water, peel the tomatoes, and chop.

Heat the olive oil in a large skillet. Add the onion, cover, and sauté over low heat for 10 minutes. Add the garlic and the basil, cover, and continue cooking for 5 minutes. Add the wine and the sugar, and cook until the liquid is reduced by half. Add the tomatoes, salt, and pepper, and simmer for 20 minutes. (Simmer longer to further reduce and intensify the flavor.) Add the lemon juice 3 minutes before the sauce is done.

Cook the linguine according to the package directions. Serve with the sauce. Garnish with freshly grated Parmesan cheese, if desired.

Turkey-Stuffed Peppers

YIELD: 4 SERVINGS

4 large heirloom sweet peppers, such as Bull Nose

2 tablespoons olive oil

1 pound ground turkey

½ cup chopped onion

2 heirloom tomatoes, chopped

¾ cup water

½ cup uncooked rice

½ tablespoon herbes de Provence

Salt and pepper, to taste

Dash of hot sauce

Breadcrumbs

Grated Parmesan cheese

❖ Cut the tops off the peppers, and remove the seeds and membrane. Place the peppers in a stockpot of boiling water for 3 minutes. Remove from the water, and invert on paper towels to drain.

Heat the olive oil in a large skillet. Add the turkey and onion. Cook until the turkey is browned and the onion is tender, then drain. Add the tomatoes, water, uncooked rice, herbs, salt, pepper, and hot sauce. Bring to a boil, then reduce heat and simmer covered for 15 minutes or until the rice is tender.

Preheat the oven to 375°F.

Fill the peppers with the meat mixture. Place in a 2-quart baking dish. Place any leftover meat mixture in the dish along with the filled peppers. Bake 10 minutes. Top with breadcrumbs and cheese, and bake an additional 5 minutes.

HEIRLOOM: BULL NOSE PEPPER

An heirloom from India, Bull Nose (also known as Large Bell or Sweet Mountain) was introduced to the American colonies in 1759. Its unique taste is a combination of sweet and heat: the thick flesh is sweet, and the ribs are slightly hot and pungent. The fruits ripen from green to scarlet and are uniform in size and shape, about 3½ inches around and 4 inches long—excellent for stuffing.

Gnocchi with Fresh Garden Pesto

YIELD: 6 SERVINGS

3 pounds heirloom russet potatoes, such as Russet Burbank

2 cups unbleached all-purpose flour

1 large farmstead egg

⅓ cup Parmesan cheese

1 cup chopped cilantro

Salt and white pepper, to taste

½ cup extra-virgin olive oil

Garden pesto

GARDEN PESTO (2 CUPS)

1 cup macadamia nuts

4 cloves garlic

1 cup cilantro leaves

1 cup chopped mint leaves

1 cup chopped Thai basil leaves

Juice of 3 lemons

Salt and black pepper, to taste

1 cup extra-virgin olive oil

❖ Place the potatoes in a saucepan, and cover with salted water. Bring to a boil, and cook about 30 minutes or until tender. Peel and quarter the potatoes, then pass them through a ricer or grater onto a large, lightly floured cutting board.

Fill a large stockpot with 6 quarts of water and salt, and bring to a boil. Have a bowl of ice water nearby.

Form a well in the middle of the potatoes, and sprinkle with the flour. Add the egg in the middle of the well, and mix with a fork. As you are mixing, add the cheese, fresh chopped herbs, salt, pepper, and olive oil. Work the mixture until it reaches a smooth consistency. Knead the dough until it is dry enough so that it does not stick to the cutting board. Be careful not to over-work the dough.

Roll the dough into cigar shapes, and cut into small pieces. Mark the pieces with a fork, and place in boiling water. When gnocchi are done, they will float to the top. Remove them from the water, and dip in the ice water to stop the cooking process.

Serve with fresh Garden Pesto.

GARDEN PESTO

This is a great recipe to make midseason, when there are lots of fresh herbs to pick. Pesto can be frozen for up to six months.

In a food processor, combine the macadamia nuts, garlic, cilantro, mint, basil, lemon juice, salt, and pepper. Puree for 2 minutes, adding the olive oil in a slow drizzle.

HEIRLOOM: RUSSET BURBANK POTATO

The most widely grown potato in the United States happens to be an heirloom—and the variety that made Idaho famous. The Russet Burbank was developed by legendary plant breeder Luther Burbank in 1874. Its reddish brown skin, white flesh, and shallow eyes make for a perfect baking or frying potato.

Baked Sea Bass with New Peas and Fava Beans

YIELD: 4 TO 6 SERVINGS

1½ cups shelled fresh fava beans

2 pounds sea bass or other white fish fillets at least 1-inch-thick, skinned, deboned, and cut into 12 equal slices

Seasoning salt

Freshly ground black pepper

½ cup extra-virgin olive oil

3 tablespoons dry white wine (such as chardonnay)

1 tablespoon chopped fresh dill

2 tablespoons minced fresh basil leaves

1½ cups shelled fresh heirloom green peas, such as Champion of England

½ cup seeded and coarsely chopped heirloom paste tomatoes

2 tablespoons freshly squeezed lemon or lime juice

1 tablespoon whole grain or Dijon mustard

Fresh basil for garnish

❖ Preheat the oven to 325°F.

Bring a medium-size heavy pot of water to a boil, and drop in the fava beans. Parboil for about 4 minutes. Drain and peel the skin from each, then set aside.

Rinse the fish in running water, and pat dry with paper towels. Season the fillets with the seasoning salt and pepper. Arrange the fish in a single layer in an oven-proof baking dish, and pierce each fillet a couple of times with a sharp-tined fork. Drizzle the oil and wine over the fillets, and sprinkle with the dill, basil, fava beans, peas, and chopped tomato. Cover with aluminum foil, and bake about 10 minutes or until the fillets flake when the point of a knife is inserted in the center. Remove the dish, and place the fillets and vegetables on a warm serving platter.

Pour the juices from the dish into a small pot, and add the juice from the lemon or lime and the mustard. Stir over medium heat until the juices slightly thicken. Pour the sauce over the fish on the serving platter. Scatter the vegetables over the fish, and garnish the platter with fresh basil.

Salad Cucumbers

❚❙❚

YIELD: 8 TO 10 SERVINGS

3 to 4 heirloom cucumbers, such as Suyo Long, peeled and thinly sliced

2 medium red heirloom onions, such as Red Torpedo, thinly sliced

½ cup white wine vinegar

½ cup water

¼ to ¾ cup sugar, to taste

½ teaspoon sea salt

❖ Slice the cucumbers and onions, and place them in a large mixing bowl. Combine the vinegar, water, sugar, and salt in a small bowl. Pour the mixture over the cucumbers and onions. Refrigerate at least overnight. Taste and adjust sugar. (You can also adjust the amount of vinegar to make the dressing more acidic.)

HEIRLOOM: SUYO LONG CUCUMBER

Cucumbers, which have been cultivated for more than 3,000 years, came to the New World with the first European explorers. Heirloom cucumber varieties, unlike the cucumbers found in the grocery, vary in shape and size from small, round, and prickly fruits to long, smooth types with few seeds. Cucumbers are classified as either pickling varieties or slicing varieties, but some are versatile enough to be used for both, as is the Suyo Long. Suyo Long, which originated in China, is sweet and burpless, that is, mild and easy on the digestive system. The fruit is long and straight with dark green ridged skin and few seeds. It is crisp and tender with a fine flavor—perfect for slicing or eating straight out of hand.

Zucchini and Tomato au Gratin

YIELD: 4 SERVINGS

1 tablespoon canola oil

½ medium onion, diced

4 medium zucchini, such as Cocozelle, cut into 1/4-inch slices

2 medium heirloom tomatoes, peeled and chopped

Salt and pepper, to taste

4 large basil leaves, chopped

¼ cup shredded cheddar cheese

❖ Preheat the oven to 375°F.

Grease a 2½-quart baking dish.

Heat the oil in a large skillet. Add the onion, and sauté until tender. Stir in the zucchini slices, and cook for 5 minutes, stirring frequently. Add the chopped tomato, salt, pepper, and basil. Cook 5 minutes longer.

Spoon the mixture into the prepared baking dish. Add the cheddar cheese. Bake 5 minutes or until the cheese melts.

Corn Fritters

YIELD: 4 TO 6 SERVINGS

½ cup unbleached all-purpose flour

2 teaspoons baking powder

½ teaspoon seasoned salt

¼ teaspoon black pepper

1 tablespoon sugar

2 large farmstead eggs

½ cup milk

1 tablespoon vegetable oil

2 cups fresh heirloom sweet corn, such as Golden Bantam, removed from the cob

❖ Combine the flour, baking powder, seasoned salt, pepper, and sugar in a large bowl. Stir in the eggs one at a time, then stir in the milk and the oil. Fold in the corn.

Heat the vegetable oil in a large skillet until hot, then reduce heat to medium. Drop tablespoons of batter into the skillet. Cook until browned on all sides, turning frequently.

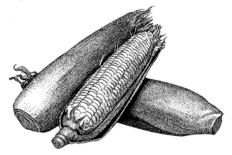

Lemon Cucumber Raita

Serve this refreshing summer side dish with meats, pita bread, or spooned over more lemon cucumbers.

YIELD: 6 SERVINGS

2 cups plain yogurt

½ cup (about 1 small fruit) grated, peeled True Lemon cucumbers

1 teaspoon sugar

½ teaspoon salt

Cracked pepper, to taste

1 clove garlic, crushed or minced

1 tablespoon crushed or torn fresh mint

❖ Place the yogurt in a medium bowl. Add the cucumber, sugar, salt, pepper, garlic, and mint. Allow to sit for 30 minutes before serving.

HEIRLOOM: TRUE LEMON CUCUMBER

Introduced in 1894 by Samuel Wilson of Pennsylvania, this unusual and unique cucumber resembles a lemon. It is small and spherical, about 3 inches by 2 inches at harvest, with white skin and bright yellow streaks. A Lemon cucumber doesn't require paring because its skin is quite thin and lacks bitterness—perfect for eating out of hand. Because its crisp white flesh is mild, the variety is considered burpless. Lemon cucumbers are versatile enough to be used for pickling or slicing.

LEMON CUCUMBER RAITA

Currant Tomato Salad

❦❦❦

YIELD: 4 SERVINGS

1 shallot

Salt and pepper, to taste

2 tablespoons red wine vinegar

1 clove garlic, minced

1 large heirloom tomato, finely chopped, juice reserved to
 make 1 cup

2 cups currants or halved cherry tomatoes

3 to 4 basil leaves

❖ Dice the shallot and place in a medium-size bowl. Add a pinch of salt, and cover with the vinegar. Let stand for 15 minutes, then strain the shallot and reserve the vinegar. Add the garlic and the heirloom tomato to the shallot. Mix well. Let stand for 15 minutes, and add salt and pepper as needed. Add some or all of the reserved vinegar if the tomatoes need acidity.

Place the halved tomatoes and the basil on a serving platter. Top with the sauce and serve.

CURRANT TOMATOES

Currant tomatoes are close to the wild tomatoes discovered by European explorers in centuries past, and all garden varieties today are crosses or selections of wild forms. The tiny currant tomato is a distinct species with characteristics—such as smaller leaves and flowers—that differ from those of the larger tomato varieties. The diminutive fruits (roughly ½ inch to 1 inch across) are abundant and hang in grape-like clusters. Currants produce an intense flavor—crisp, sweet, and sometimes tart. They are excellent whole in salads and prove especially interesting when red and yellow varieties are used in combination.

Heirloom Tomato Salad

This quintessential summer salad lets the tomatoes do the talking. Don't bother making this dish in any other season; the tomatoes just aren't good enough. For best results, use only tomatoes fresh off the vine from your own yard, from a generous friend's, or from the farmers market. For a more substantial offering, you can top with fresh crumbled goat cheese and serve with a French baguette.

YIELD: 4 TO 6 SERVINGS

2 pounds heirloom red, yellow, or striped slicing tomatoes
   of various sizes and shapes

1 small red onion, finely chopped

1 bunch basil, coarsely chopped (reserve about 10 sprigs for
   garnish)

Extra-virgin olive oil

Red wine vinegar

Fresh coarsely ground black pepper, to taste

Fresh coarsely ground kosher sea salt, to taste

❖ Cut the tomatoes into slices, and place in two layers on a large plate. Sprinkle the tomatoes evenly with the red onion and the chopped basil. Generously dribble the olive oil over the tomatoes, followed by the vinegar. (The ratio should be about 1 part vinegar to 4 parts olive oil.) Add salt and pepper to taste.

Prepare this salad about one-half hour before serving to allow flavors to meld.

Spicy Cool Mexican Salad

This is the ultimate Mexican salad—made with avocado, corn, chili pepper, and lime. For extra spiciness, leave the seeds in the jalapeño.

YIELD: 8 TO 10 SERVINGS

2 medium-size avocados, peeled, pitted, and chopped into
  small chunks

1 cup fresh sweet-corn kernels, cut from cobs, sautéed, and
  cooled

½ cup chopped cilantro

1 jalapeño pepper, seeded and minced

2 medium-size red heirloom tomatoes, chopped coarsely

1 medium-size sweet onion, chopped coarsely

Juice from 1 large lime

¼ cup olive oil

½ teaspoon salt

½ teaspoon black pepper

½ teaspoon chili pepper

❖ Toss together all ingredients in a large bowl. Refrigerate for 30 minutes before serving.

Marinated Beans with Tomatoes

YIELD: 4 TO 6 SERVINGS

1½ pounds heirloom snap beans, such as Burpee's
     Stringless Green Pod, ends trimmed

1 bunch chives, finely chopped

¾ cup red wine vinegar

¾ cup extra-virgin olive oil

¼ cup plus 1 tablespoon sugar

1 teaspoon Hungarian paprika

4 cloves garlic, minced

1 teaspoon salt

1 teaspoon black pepper

2 medium-size heirloom tomatoes, coarsely chopped

Bring 1 gallon heavily salted water to a boil. Add the beans and cook 5 to 6 minutes. Strain the beans and rinse with cold water.

Combine the finely chopped chives, red wine vinegar, olive oil, sugar, paprika, minced garlic, salt, and pepper to make the dressing.

❖ In a medium-size bowl, combine the tomatoes and beans. Pour the dressing over the bean mixture, and stir gently to mix.

Refrigerate and allow to sit for at least 3 hours (the longer the better), stirring every hour or so.

HEIRLOOM:
BURPEE'S STRINGLESS GREEN POD

Snap beans come in many shapes and sizes, but snap refers to how the beans are used—the young pods are eaten fresh. Most home gardeners prefer snap varieties that are stringless, that is, lacking tough fiber (parchment) in the young pods.

Burpee's Stringless Green Pod is a snap bush bean that was developed in 1894 by Calvin Keeney, a notorious bean breeder also known as the father of the stringless bean. Burpee's Stringless Green Pod beans are 5 to 6 inches long and curved, with a meaty, juicy, exceptional flavor.

Stuffed Heirloom Tomatoes

This recipe does not utilize specific measurements, as it was written to be easily adjusted to suit individual tastes.

‖♀

YIELD: DEPENDS ON NUMBER OF TOMATOES USED

Olive oil

Medium- to large-size heirloom tomatoes of different colors and shapes, such as Green Zebra, Mr. Charlie, Yellow Stuffer, Amana Orange, and Brandywine

Salt and pepper, to taste

Chopped mushrooms

Butter

Chopped shallots

Garlic

Pine nuts

Italian parsley

White wine

Finely chopped cooked ham

Breadcrumbs

Grated Parmesan cheese

❖ Preheat the oven to 350°F.

Lightly grease a baking sheet.

Remove the stem on each tomato, and open the top gently. Press lightly to remove the juice and seeds. Season the inside of the tomatoes with salt and pepper to taste. Set on the prepared baking sheet. Pour a few drops of olive oil into each tomato, and place in the oven for 5 minutes. Remove from the oven and drain the tomatoes.

In a sauté pan, brown the mushrooms, shallots, garlic, pine nuts, and parsley in butter and olive oil. Moisten with white wine. Remove the mushroom mixture from the heat.

Combine the ham and breadcrumbs with the mushroom mixture. Stuff the mixture into each tomato. Top with more breadcrumbs mixed with Parmesan cheese piled in a dome into each tomato. Return the tomatoes to the baking sheet, and sprinkle with olive oil.

Bake 12 to 15 minutes.

Tomato Tart

Puff pastry is easy to use, inexpensive, and gives a tart, elegant but rustic feel to the dish.

YIELD: 4 SERVINGS

1 frozen puff pastry

⅓ cup soft goat cheese

4 medium heirloom tomatoes, two red and two yellow, sliced ¼ inch thick

¼ small red onion, thinly sliced

½ cup coarsely chopped basil leaves

1 clove garlic

Salt and pepper, to taste

¼ cup kalamata olives (optional)

1 tablespoon capers (optional)

¼ cup extra-virgin olive oil

❖ Allow the pastry to thaw about 20 minutes before assembling the tart. Once thawed, unfold the pastry—you can smooth any crease with a bit of water on your fingertips. Place on a small greased baking sheet.

Preheat the oven to 400°F.

Spread the goat cheese in the center of the pastry, leaving about a 2-inch margin at the edge. Pile the tomato slices over the goat cheese, then top with the red onion slices. Fold the pastry around the edges to meet the filling, creating a sort of boat. It doesn't have to look perfect. Sprinkle the filling with the basil, garlic, salt, and pepper. Add olives and capers, if desired. Cover with olive oil.

Bake 20 to 25 minutes or until the crust is golden brown. You can serve the tart whole or cut into wedges.

Sesame Rattlesnake Pole Beans

YIELD: 6 SERVINGS

1 pound cleaned and trimmed heirloom Rattlesnake pole beans (or substitute with flat Italian beans)

1 teaspoon kosher salt

1 tablespoon toasted sesame oil

1 tablespoon toasted sesame seeds

❖ Heat 2 quarts of heavily salted water in a large stockpot and bring to a boil. Drop the beans into the boiling water, and simmer for 8 to 10 minutes.

Drain the beans, and plunge them into a bowl filled with ice water to stop the cooking process. Place in a serving bowl. Sprinkle with the salt, sesame oil, and sesame seeds, tossing to coat the beans evenly. Serve cold or at room temperature.

HEIRLOOM: RATTLESNAKE BEAN

The Rattlesnake bean is a snap pole bean with dark green pods mottled with purple streaks, looking somewhat like the skin on a rattlesnake. It is sometimes called the preacher bean because of its high productivity, which is something to preach about. Rattlesnake beans produce beautiful buff-colored seeds speckled with dark brown markings. The tender seeds have a good bean flavor and make a hearty soup or salad.

Zucchini Cake

This old favorite is delightful and refreshing served with lemon sorbet.

YIELD: 8 TO 10 SERVINGS

1 cup vegetable oil

2 cups sugar

3 large farmstead eggs

3 cups unbleached all-purpose flour

1 teaspoon baking powder

1 teaspoon baking soda

1 teaspoon salt

2 cups mashed, cooked heirloom zucchini, such as Black Zucchini

½ cup raisins

2 teaspoons vanilla

½ cup chopped pecans, lightly toasted

❖ Preheat the oven to 350°F.

Lightly grease and flour a 9 x 13–inch baking pan.

Cream the oil and sugar in a medium bowl. Add the eggs and mix well.

Sift the flour, baking powder, baking soda, and salt in a large bowl. Combine creamed mixture with the dry ingredients. Fold in the zucchini, raisins, vanilla, and pecans. Pour into the prepared baking pan.

Bake 30 minutes and allow to cool before slicing.

Cherry Cobbler

YIELD: 12 SERVINGS

2 sticks plus 2 tablespoons butter

3½ cups unbleached all-purpose flour, divided

1 cup sugar

1 teaspoon baking powder

1 large farmstead egg, beaten

4 cups pitted heirloom tart cherries, such as Montmorency

½ cup confectioners' sugar

❖ Preheat the oven to 350°F.

Combine one stick of butter, 2 cups of flour, sugar, baking powder, and egg in a large bowl and mix well. Press into the bottom of a 9 × 13–inch baking pan. Cover with the cherries.

Use your hands to mix the remaining butter, flour, and confectioners' sugar in a medium bowl until it's crumbly. Sprinkle over the cherries.

Bake 45 minutes.

HOME ORCHARDS

If you think of orchard fruits as only mass-produced commercial crops, think again. Small orchards have been a significant part of North American horticulture since the 1700s. Eighteenth-century homesteaders often commenced planting their orchards before constructing their dwellings. In fact, for most early Americans, horticulture meant fruit growing, rather than vegetable growing.

If you're thinking of planting an orchard, consider cherry trees. Cherries are a practical fruit for home orchards where the climate and soil conditions are suitable—moderately cool summers with low humidity and sandy or well-draining soil. Once cherry trees are established, they require little maintenance and are reliable producers. You can expect a harvest in the fourth or fifth year after planting. And with pruning, you can keep your tree to any size.

Consider growing the Montmorency tart cherry. Tart, or sour, cherries are rarely sold in grocery stores, but they are the key ingredient in desserts—pies and cobblers. Montmorency dates back to the 1400s and has been grown in the United States for over a century. Sour cherry trees are smaller than sweet cherry trees are, but they are reliable producers.

CHERRY COBBLER

SUMMER RASPBERRY CHEESECAKE

Summer Raspberry Cheesecake

The Neufchâtel cheese gives this luscious dessert a lighter texture than if you used standard cream cheese. This cheesecake takes some time to make, but it is definitely worth the effort.

‖†‖

YIELD: 8 TO 10 SERVINGS

CRUST

1¾ cups crushed graham crackers

¼ cup finely chopped almonds

½ teaspoon ground cinnamon

½ cup butter, melted

FILLING

2 8-ounce packages cream cheese, softened to room temperature

8 ounces Neufchâtel cheese, softened to room temperature

1 cup finely ground raw cane sugar

2 tablespoons unbleached all-purpose flour

1 teaspoon vanilla extract

½ teaspoon finely shredded orange peel (optional)

2 large farmstead eggs

1 large farmstead egg yolk

¼ cup whole milk

1 cup washed fresh whole heirloom raspberries, such as Caroline raspberries

CRUST

❖ Combine the graham crackers, almonds, and cinnamon in a medium bowl, and stir in the melted butter. Press the mixture into the bottom and sides of a lightly greased 8-inch springform pan. Place the crust in the refrigerator to chill for 20 to 30 minutes.

FILLING

Preheat the oven to 375°F.

Beat the cream cheese and Neufchâtel cheese in a large mixing bowl until well mixed. Add the raw sugar, flour, vanilla extract, and orange peel (if desired), and beat until well combined. Add the eggs and egg yolk, and beat until combined. Stir in the milk until well blended, then fold in the raspberries. Pour the filling into the chilled crust, and place on a baking sheet.

Bake for 35 to 40 minutes, then reduce the oven temperature to 200°F, and bake 10 to 15 minutes longer or until the center appears set.

Remove the cheesecake from the oven, and set on a wire rack. Let cool for 15 minutes. Using a knife, carefully loosen crust from the sides of the pan, and let cool another 30 minutes. Remove the sides of the pan, and chill in the refrigerator for 4 hours before serving.

Serve with freshly whipped cream (optional) and fresh raspberries.

RASPBERRIES

The raspberry is an herbaceous plant belonging to the rose family. Two types exist: June-bearing (or summer-bearing) raspberries are plants that carry one heavy crop of fruit during the summer months; fall-bearing (or everbearing) plants have a longer harvest season than the summer bearers do, and they bear fruit until late September or later. A single cultivar cannot be universally recommended, but Caroline is considered the new standard for fall-bearing raspberries. Though not an heirloom, it is a vigorous early fruiting plant widely adapted for areas from the East Coast to the West Coast. It produces large firm red fruit with a rich and intense raspberry flavor.

Stone Fruit Ice Cream

Why bother with the oven if you can enjoy summer fruit cold and without an ounce of effort? Stone fruit ice cream hits the spot on a warm summer day.

YIELD: 4 TO 6 SERVINGS

4 cups peeled, pitted, quartered stone fruit (peaches, plums, or apricots)

1 cup sugar

3 large egg yolks

1 cup whole milk

1 cup heavy or whipping cream

❖ Blend all the ingredients in a blender. Pour into an ice cream maker, and then follow the manufacturer's directions.

Lemon Bars

YIELD: 16 TO 20 SQUARES

1 cup unbleached all-purpose flour

½ cup softened unsalted butter or margarine

¼ cup confectioners' sugar

2 large farmstead eggs

1 cup sugar

½ teaspoon baking powder

¼ teaspoon finely ground kosher salt

2 tablespoons fresh-squeezed Meyer lemon juice

Additional confectioners' sugar (optional)

❖ Preheat the oven to 350°F.

Combine the flour, butter, and confectioners' sugar in a medium bowl, and mix well. Press the mixture into an ungreased 8 × 8–inch baking pan, building up the edge about 1/2 inch on the sides of the pan. Bake 20 minutes or until lightly golden. Remove from the oven, and set aside.

Combine the eggs, sugar, baking powder, kosher salt, and lemon juice, and beat for about 3 minutes or until light and fluffy. Pour the mixture over the warm crust.

Bake about 25 minutes or until no imprint remains when the lemon mixture is touched in the center. Cool completely. Sprinkle with additional confectioners' sugar if desired. Cut into squares.

STONE FRUIT ICE CREAM

FALL

 Fall is arguably the most splendid of seasons. The leaves are turning glorious shades of gold, orange, and red, carpeting the earth in jewel tones. Days are still warm but with a crisp chill in the evening air. For the first time in months, we begin to think about gloves, jackets, and warm hats.

The growing season is slowly winding down, but it's not time to relax just yet. The last of the harvest is being picked and preserved; seeds are still being saved, dried, and stored; and beds are being mulched and prepared for their cold winter nap. We dig deep and plan for spring by planting bulbs of tulips, crocuses, and daffodils; their cold slumber will prepare them for bloom.

The hobby-farm kitchen is scented with the spices and the aromas of fall—cinnamon, allspice, clove, and nutmeg—as we prepare our favorite dishes of winter squash, pumpkins, and apples with fruits newly harvested from the fields. We anticipate the holidays and begin planning for one or more family gatherings—a good time to dig out the heirloom recipes or research new ones and try them out before the big day.

JOHN MITCHELL

HEIRLOOM HARVEST
COMMUNITY FARM AND CSA

John Mitchell is passionate about heirloom varieties, albeit in a cautious and thoughtful manner. "Heirloom varieties are cultural artifacts," he explains. "They represent generations of knowledge, the efforts of farmers and gardeners who have come before us. We are at r sk right now of losing many of them because of standardization and through the loss of small seed companies that make these lines available to gardeners and growers."

On his farm in Westborough, Massachusetts, John has set about preserving heirloom varieties, as well as the precious farmland on which they're grown. As a relatively young farmer, John transitioned into full-time farming from his former profession as a journalist in 1999. But farming is not easy in Westborough—a town that lies thirty-two miles west of Boston and that ranks number one on the Massachusetts Audubon Society's list of farmlands being converted to housing tracts. "I really feel I'm on the frontline here," he says.

John's seventeen-acre certified organic Heirloom Harvest Community Farm and CSA is under long-term lease from the town's Catholic parish. Without such an arrangement, he believes the land would have been filled with houses long ago. He's determined to keep the land in cultivation, and he's learned one key technique for building public support for his cause from the land trust movement—get people's feet on the farmland itself. "It has to be real, not abstract," he explains. "They have to have a relationship with it in order to care to save it." That is why Heirloom Harvest is open to the public and its community-supported agriculture business is booming. "CSA is a great model for reconnecting suburbanites to what's left of the agricultural landscape around them."

John grows more than fifty varieties of vegetables and fruits, with about 35 percent of his crop in heirlooms; the others are modern varieties and hybrids that meet organic-certification guidelines. He changes his mix of crops yearly because "there are some rarer crops that people just don't want to get every year." His goal is to someday grow heirloom varieties entirely, but he's also a pragmatic businessman. He believes his farm should produce abundantly to repay his CSA members' investment. So each year John tests new heirlooms to determine whether they will perform reliably enough to replace a modern variety in his crop plan. "I couldn't just jump in with an all-heirloom crop plan that might have resulted in massive failure of untested varieties or an uneven harvest," he explains. "Also, just because something is old doesn't mean it is desirable. Even heirlooms can be dull and insipid."

Heirloom Harvest Community Farm's CSA shares have sold out every year John has been in business, with two-thirds of his members living locally and the other third coming from as far away as Rhode Island and Connecticut. He was lucky enough to have inherited a local following from the previous farmer of the land. Having farmed this site for four years, John realizes that because different farms have different characteristics (such as water, soil, elevation, drainage, and wind), it takes at least five years to learn to farm a specific site well. "When you farm organically without the crutch of synthetic chemicals, it is even more challenging," he says. "And when you're growing heirlooms, you introduce another element of unpredictability and risk." Because Americans today are exposed to so little of what is actually possible and available—the flavors, the textures, the colors, and the smells—it's no wonder, John says, that kids don't eat their vegetables. "Heirlooms are the last, perhaps lost, frontier of food variety and taste."

Heirloom Harvest Community Farm and CSA
PO Box 1031
Westborough, MA 01581
(508) 963-7792
http://www.heirloomharvestcsa.com

Red Wine Onions

This onion "jam" is especially flavorful when made with heirloom onions such as Southport White Globe, a medium-size white onion with a fairly mild flavor. It is excellent served with creamy cheeses such as Brie, Camembert, and Morbier on a cheese plate with crusty bread or even with red meats or potato pancakes.

YIELD: 10 TO 12 SERVINGS

4 medium white heirloom onions, such as Southport White Globe or White Portugal

4 tablespoons olive oil

1 tablespoon sea salt

4 bay leaves

¼ cup honey

½ cup red wine vinegar

½ cup balsamic vinegar

½ cup red wine

Coarsely ground pepper, to taste

❖ Peel the onions, and cut them in half. Slice the onions with the grain as thinly as possible.

Heat the olive oil in a large saucepan or dutch oven over high heat until the oil is very hot, almost smoking. Add the onions, and cook a minute or so without stirring to allow some of the onions to brown slightly. Then stir well, and add the salt and bay leaves. Reduce the heat to medium, and continue to cook the onions, stirring constantly to allow the onions to brown or at least cook through, about 30 to 35 minutes. Add the honey and cook another minute or two, being careful not to burn the onions. Add the vinegars and red wine, and bring to a boil. Turn the heat to low, and allow the vinegars and wine to reduce, about 45 minutes.

Once all the liquid has evaporated, remove the onions from the heat, and season with black pepper. Add more salt, honey, or vinegar to achieve desired flavor. Remove bay leaves before serving.

Creamy Fall Vegetable Soup

YIELD: 6 TO 8 SERVINGS

2 tablespoons olive oil

2 cups yellow heirloom onions, such as Australian Brown, peeled and diced

Salt and white pepper, to taste

2 pounds heirloom parsnips, such as The Student, peeled and diced

1 pound potatoes, peeled and diced

1 tablespoon chopped garlic

8 cups chicken stock

½ to 1 cup heavy cream

Chopped fresh parsley and/or parboiled carrots, thinly sliced for garnish

❖ In a heavy-bottomed stockpot, heat the oil over medium-high heat. Add the onions, and season with salt and pepper. Sauté for 2 to 3 minutes or until soft. Add the parsnips, potatoes, and garlic, and season with additional salt and pepper to taste. Stir in the stock, and bring to a boil over medium-high heat. Reduce the heat to a simmer, and continue to cook for 1 hour or until the vegetables are tender, stirring occasionally. Remove from the heat.

Using a blender and working in batches, puree the soup until smooth. Slowly stir in the cream. Add salt and pepper, if needed.

Ladle soup into individual serving bowls, and garnish with parsley, carrots, or both.

RED WINE ONIONS

Poached Pears with Minted Goat Cheese

YIELD: 18 APPETIZERS

3 heirloom pears, such as Bloodgood, Colonel Wilder, or Dorset

6 cups water

1 cup white wine

3 cups sugar

1 tablespoon chopped fresh ginger

2 whole cloves

1 cinnamon stick

1 French baguette

½ cup olive oil, divided

2 cups softened goat cheese

2 tablespoons minced fresh mint

❖ Peel the pears and place in a large saucepan. Add the water, wine, sugar, ginger, cloves, and cinnamon stick. Bring to a simmer over medium-low heat, and stir occasionally, making sure the pears are fully sub-merged. (The pears will float, so they must be stirred often.) Cook 20 to 30 minutes or until the flesh is soft but not mushy. Strain the pears from the liquid, and allow to cool in the refrigerator for about 1 hour. When cool, dice the pears into small pieces.

Preheat the oven to 350°F.

Cut the baguette in ½-inch slices on the bias. Lightly brush with olive oil, and place on a baking sheet. Bake the bread slices for 7 to 10 minutes or until golden and toasted through.

Mix the softened goat cheese with 2 tablespoons of the olive oil in a small bowl. Mix until smooth. Add the chopped mint. Place the mixture in a pastry bag with a small star tip. Pipe about ½ to 1 tablespoon goat cheese mixture onto each bread slice. Mound about ½ tablespoon of diced pear on the goat cheese. Serve immediately.

HEIRLOOM:
AMERICAN HEIRLOOM PEARS

American heirloom pears are considered rare nineteenth- and twentieth-century varieties of American origin. The thirty-two different varieties listed on Slow Food USA's Ark of Taste—including Bloodgood, Colonel Wilder, and Dorset—vary from pale yellow to deep brownish yellow in color and from large to petite in size. Tastes range from sweet to spicy, and textures vary from gritty to smooth.

Pear cuttings were first brought to the New World from Europe. Early colonists used the fruit for eating and baking, the fine-grained wood for making furniture, and the leaves for making yellow dye. To the west, the Spanish brought pears to Mexico, Peru, and Chile. Later, the Spanish brought them up the California coast with the early Spanish missions.

California became a major pear-producing state in the late 1800s, after the gold rush, when farmers planted large orchards of European varieties to provide fruits for the rapidly growing population. Consumers enjoyed fresh fruit from their local markets up until World War II. After the war, the small and easily bruised heritage varieties were gradually replaced by the Bartlett, a large pear that could withstand shipping and handling and had a long shelf life.

The decreasing diversity of pear varieties in the United States and worldwide is significant. Sources for previously abundant pear cuttings have rapidly disappeared, and commercial orchardists who once took pride in growing many varieties of pears now confine their efforts to just a few.

Sweet Potato and Apple Soup

YIELD: 10 SERVINGS

1 tablespoon unsalted butter

1 tablespoon olive oil

1 large heirloom onion, such as Ailsa Craig Exhibition,
   peeled and diced

2 shallots, peeled and minced

2 pounds heirloom sweet potatoes, such as Southern Queen,
   peeled and cut in cubes

½ pound carrots, peeled and cut in cubes

2 tart heirloom apples, such as Newtown Pippin, peeled,
   cored, and cut in cubes

½ ripe papaya, peeled, seeded, and cut in cubes

3 cups chicken stock

1 cup water

½ cup crème fraîche*

Bunch fresh thyme

❖ Melt the butter in a large stockpot, and add the olive oil. Add the onion and shallots, and sauté over medium heat for 3 to 5 minutes. Reduce the heat; add the sweet potatoes, carrots, apples, and papaya; and continue to sauté for an additional 8 minutes, stirring frequently. Add the chicken stock and water. Simmer, covered, for 30 minutes or until the vegetables and fruits are soft.

Transfer the soup to a food processor in batches and puree. Return the soup to a saucepan, blend well, and reheat if necessary. Thin with a bit more stock if the soup is too thick.

Serve garnished with a dollop of crème fraîche and a sprig of fresh thyme.

* If crème fraîche is not readily available, use 2 cups of heavy cream—do not use ultrapasteurized heavy cream—with 4 tablespoons buttermilk. Set aside at room temperature for 10 to 24 hours, then refrigerate. It will thicken in two days.

HEIRLOOM:
SOUTHERN QUEEN SWEET POTATO

The sweet potato is a morning glory—a tropical plant that thrives in a warm, sunny climate and requires a long growing season. The sweet potato is not related botanically to the yam or the common potato (see Sweet Potatoes Versus Yams on page 170).

Southern Queen is a nineteenth-century variety that was introduced from South America in 1870 and has stood the test of time. One of the oldest varieties grown in the United States, the Southern Queen tuber has white skin with dry, sweet white flesh.

Spicy Pumpkin Soup

For this recipe, use the smaller, sweet varieties of pumpkins such as Small Sugar.

YIELD: 4 TO 6 SERVINGS

¼ cup minced shallot

½ cup minced white onion

2 tablespoons butter

2 cups roasted, diced, and pureed heirloom pumpkin, such as Small Sugar

4 cups chicken broth

½ teaspoon red pepper flakes

1 teaspoon paprika

Salt and pepper, to taste

1 cup half-and-half

Minced parsley for garnish

❖ In a large saucepan, sauté the shallot and the onion in butter until translucent. Add the pumpkin, chicken broth, red pepper flakes, paprika, and the salt and pepper to taste. Simmer 15 minutes. Cool slightly, then puree the soup in a blender in batches or use a handheld blender. Return the soup to the pan, and add the half-and-half. Simmer 5 to 10 minutes (do not boil). Adjust seasoning as needed.

Spoon the soup into individual bowls, and garnish with minced parsley.

HEIRLOOM: SMALL SUGAR PUMPKIN

Considered perhaps the best all-around pumpkin and the traditional favorite of home gardeners, the Small Sugar (also known as New England Pie) was introduced in America before 1860. Native Americans gave the seeds to early colonists, who considered them an essential winter foodstuff, their tough skin making them perfect for winter storage. The Small Sugar pumpkin is a small, as its name implies (6 to 8 pounds), orange, ribbed globe with slightly flattened ends. It has thick, fine-grained, stringless, and sweet flesh perfect for baking into pies, for canning, and for fortifying soups.

Corn and Sausage Chowder

This rich chowder combines the best of farm-fresh ingredients: vegetables, meat, and dairy. Add a crusty loaf of bread or a simple green salad for a hearty meal.

YIELD: 4 TO 6 SERVINGS

1¼ pounds hot Italian sausage

½ cup butter

1½ cups diced heirloom onion, such as Yellow Ebenezer

1 cup diced celery

5 cups chicken broth, divided

3 cups peeled and diced heirloom potatoes, such as Garnet Chili or Bintje

⅓ cup unbleached all-purpose flour

3 cups fresh heirloom corn, such as Golden Bantam

½ teaspoon salt

1 cup half-and-half

1 cup heavy cream

❖ In a dutch oven or large, heavy saucepan, brown the sausage, then remove from the pan and set aside. Melt the butter in the pan along with the sausage drippings. Add the onion and celery. Stir and sauté for 5 minutes or until the vegetables are softened. Add 4 cups of the chicken broth and the potatoes; cover and bring to a boil over medium-high heat. Reduce the heat to medium, and simmer, covered, until the potatoes are just tender, about 15 minutes.

In a small bowl, whisk together the remaining cup of chicken broth and the flour until smooth.

Increase the heat under the vegetable-broth mixture, and bring just to a boil. Gradually stir in the flour mixture. Stir in the corn, and simmer for 3 to 4 minutes or until the corn is tender. Add the sausage to the vegetable-broth mixture along with the salt, and stir to combine. Add the half-and-half and the heavy cream, and continue cooking over medium heat.

Serve immediately or keep warm over low heat. Do not boil.

APPLE SQUASH SOUP

Apple Squash Soup

The best flavor of winter squash is brought out by the high temperatures of sautéing and roasting. Dry-fleshed varieties are best for general cooking, while moist-fleshed varieties are better suited for use in pies.

YIELD: 6 TO 8 SERVINGS

3 tablespoons butter

2 cups chopped yellow heirloom onions, such as Yellow Ebenezer

2 teaspoons minced fresh garlic

1 teaspoon minced fresh ginger

1½ cups apples, peeled and chopped

4½ cups chicken broth

2 cups heirloom winter squash, such as Hubbard, cooked and cubed

¼ teaspoon cinnamon

⅛ teaspoon nutmeg

Salt and black pepper, to taste

Sour cream and apple slices for garnish

❖ Melt the butter in a heavy-bottomed saucepan over medium heat. Add the onions, garlic, and ginger, and sauté until translucent. Add the apples and chicken broth. Bring to a boil, then lower the heat, and simmer about 15 minutes or until the apples are tender. Remove from heat, and stir in the squash and spices. Working in batches, puree mixture in a blender or food processor until smooth.

To serve, reheat the soup on low heat until hot but not boiling. Garnish with a dollop of sour cream topped by fresh apple slices.

HEIRLOOM: HUBBARD SQUASH

The Hubbard is the original variety of all the popular Hubbard squashes, such as Blue Hubbard and Golden Hubbard, and it originated in the West Indies or South America. Its North American history dates to 1798, when the seed was carried from Boston to Marblehead, Massachusetts, where it was grown for many years. In 1842, seed dealer James J. H. Gregory obtained the seed after learning about it from Elizabeth Hubbard, and he named the squash in her honor. Gregory introduced the Hubbard squash to the trade in the late 1840s.

A true Hubbard should measure 12 to 15 inches in length and weigh 9 to 12 pounds. Hubbard fruits are oblong with pointed ends; their skin is dark green with a tough, wrinkled, and warty texture and a few pale green stripes. The dull yellow flesh is dry and firm, slightly sweet, and substantial—well suited for cooking.

Red Onion and Garlic Spread

This spread is best on crusty French bread and crackers, but it also works well as a seasoning for soups and sautés. Use Red Torpedo onions for their bright red flesh and spicy, tangy flavor, or Southport Red Globe for its pinkish firm flesh and pungent flavor.

YIELD: 2 CUPS

3 large bulbs garlic, with outer skin removed

½ cup extra-virgin olive oil, divided

4 heirloom red onions, chopped

2 tablespoons red wine vinegar

1 tablespoon finely grated horseradish root

2 tablespoons chopped fresh thyme

¼ teaspoon salt

Freshly ground black pepper

❖ Preheat the oven to 350°F.

Slice off the top of each garlic bulb. Place the bulbs, cut side up, on a square of aluminum foil. Drizzle the heads with ¼ cup of the olive oil, and wrap loosely, leaving the foil slightly open. Place the wrapped bulbs in a shallow roasting pan, and roast the in the oven for 45 to 60 minutes or until tender when pressed.

In a large skillet, heat the remaining oil, and sauté the chopped onions over medium heat until the onions are softened and slightly golden, about 8 minutes. Add the vinegar and horseradish, and cook for about 2 minutes. Set aside to cool.

Remove the roasted garlic from the oven, and loosen the foil. Set aside until cool enough to handle. Save the oil from the packets. Squeeze out the cooled cloves, and place in a food processor. Add the onion and pan liquid, thyme, salt, and pepper. Process to a smooth puree, and add a little bit of the reserved oil from the roasted garlic. Adjust seasoning if necessary.

The mixture can be stored in an airtight container in the refrigerator for several weeks.

Chicken Curry Soup

YIELD: 4 SERVINGS

4 free-range chicken legs-and-thigh pieces, boiled in salt
water until tender and cooled

2 tablespoons olive oil

1 large shallot, finely chopped

2 tablespoons finely chopped fresh ginger

1 large clove garlic, finely chopped

2 medium heirloom carrots, such as Chantenay, peeled and
diced

1 stalk celery, diced

1 stalk lemongrass, split in half lengthwise

6 cups vegetable broth or stock

1 cup unsweetened coconut milk

3 tablespoons curry powder

1 tablespoon red pepper flakes

5 shitake mushrooms, sliced thinly

1 cup fresh cauliflower, cut into small florets

Salt and pepper, to taste

4 cups prepared white rice

❖ Cut the meat from the chicken bones, shred, and set aside.

Heat a large stockpot over medium heat. Add the olive oil, shallot, ginger, and garlic. Cook 5 minutes, stirring often. Add the carrot and celery, and cook for 2 minutes. Add the lemongrass, then cover with the vegetable broth.

Whisk together the coconut milk and curry powder in a small bowl until smooth. Whisk the curry mixture into the vegetable broth. Add the red pepper flakes, and simmer for 5 minutes. Stir in the shitake mushrooms, the cauliflower, the chicken, and salt and pepper to taste. Simmer for 8 to 10 minutes or until the cauliflower is tender.

Remove the lemongrass stalk from the soup, and serve over rice.

Whole Wheat Carrot Pineapple Muffins

These muffins are a special morning treat served warm with cream cheese.

YIELD: 2 DOZEN MUFFINS

1 8-ounce can crushed pineapple, drained, juice reserved

⅓ to ½ cup milk

2 cups whole wheat flour

1⅓ cups packed light brown sugar

1 tablespoon baking powder

½ teaspoon salt

2 tablespoons sugar

½ teaspoon cinnamon

¾ cup finely grated carrot

⅓ cup vegetable oil

1 large farmstead egg, beaten

½ teaspoon vanilla extract

½ cup chopped walnuts (optional)

❖ Preheat the oven to 375°F.

Grease two muffin tins.

Place the pineapple juice in a glass measuring cup, and add enough milk to make ¾ cup of liquid. Transfer the mixture to a small bowl, and set aside.

In a large mixing bowl, combine the whole wheat flour, brown sugar, baking powder, salt, sugar, and cinnamon. Stir in the grated carrot and the crushed pineapple until well coated. Make a well in the center of the mixture.

In a separate bowl, combine the milk-juice mixture, oil, egg, and vanilla. Add to the well of the dry ingredients, and stir until just moistened. Add the walnuts, if desired. Spoon into the prepared muffin pans, filling each cup two-thirds full.

Bake 20 to 25 minutes or until a toothpick inserted in the center comes out clean.

WHOLE WHEAT CARROT PINEAPPLE MUFFINS

APPLE BREAD

Apple Bread

❚❙❚

YIELD: 8 SERVINGS

¼ cup shortening

1 cup sugar

2 large farmstead eggs, well beaten

2 cups unbleached all-purpose flour

1 teaspoon baking powder

1 teaspoon baking soda

½ teaspoon salt

2 cups peeled, coarsely grated heirloom apple, such as
   Baldwin

1 tablespoon finely grated lemon peel

⅔ cup chopped walnuts

❖ Preheat the oven to 350°F.

Grease and flour an 8 × 5–inch loaf pan.

Cream the shortening and sugar together until fluffy, then beat in the eggs.

Sift together the flour, baking powder, baking soda, and salt. Gradually add to the egg mixture, alternating with portions of the grated apple. Stir in the lemon peel and walnuts. The batter will be stiff. Spoon the batter into the prepared pan.

Bake 50 to 60 minutes or until a toothpick inserted in the middle comes out clean and the top is nicely browned. Cool thoroughly. Do not slice until cooled.

HEIRLOOM: ANTIQUE APPLES

Antique, or heirloom, apples sometimes look ugly by modern-day standards, but the spectrum of taste—from tart and tangy to sweet and spicy—can't be beat. These older varieties don't resemble anything you'll find in supermarkets today. Antique apples are small and often misshapen and blemished, and they don't necessarily store well. Despite their appearance, most are juicy and crisp with an aromatic, intense flavor. Hundreds of varieties exist, many cultivated long ago for a specific purpose such as cider making. A few notables include:

• Golden Russet, an American variety that dates to 1845, is comparable to fine European gourmet apples. It is suitable for cider making and fresh eating. Its rich, dense flesh is punctuated with flavors of sugar and honey.

• The Gravenstein, whose known history dates to the 1600s in Europe, is an extremely flavorful and popular apple today. The early Gravensteins are ready for harvest in July each year, and their juicy, spicy taste makes them excellent for dessert and culinary use.

• Chenango Strawberry apples originated in Chenango County, New York, in the 1800s. This variety is delicate and fragrant, reminiscent of roses.

Corn Bread

YIELD: 4 TO 6 SERVINGS

½ **pound bacon, diced**

1 cup yellow cornmeal

1 cup unbleached all-purpose flour

¼ **cup plus 2 tablespoons sugar**

1 tablespoon baking powder

1 teaspoon salt

⅓ **cup vegetable oil**

1 large farmstead egg

1 cup milk

1 cup fresh heirloom sweet corn, such as Country Gentleman (white) or Golden Bantam (yellow)

❖ Preheat the oven to 400°F.

Cook the bacon until crispy, then drain and reserve the fat. Use some of the fat to grease either a cast-iron skillet or an 8-inch baking dish.

Combine the cornmeal, flour, ¼ cup sugar, baking powder, and salt in a large mixing bowl. Combine the oil, egg, and milk in a medium bowl. Stir the wet ingredients into the dry ingredients. Add the bacon and the corn, and stir until just combined. The batter will be lumpy. Pour the batter into the prepared skillet or baking dish.

Place in the oven and bake 15 minutes.

Sprinkle the remaining 2 tablespoons sugar on top, and continue cooking for 10 minutes or until a toothpick inserted in the middle comes out clean.

Cranberry Orange Buckwheat Pancakes

YIELD: 10 TO 12 LARGE PANCAKES

1 large farmstead egg

1 cup buttermilk

2 tablespoons corn oil

½ cup buckwheat flour

½ cup unbleached all-purpose flour

1 tablespoon sugar

1 teaspoon baking powder

½ teaspoon salt

½ teaspoon baking soda

⅓ cup cooked cranberries, sweetened

⅓ cup chopped orange (or mandarin orange) segments

½ teaspoon orange extract

❖ Beat the egg in a large bowl. Add the buttermilk, oil, flours, sugar, baking powder, salt, and baking soda, and mix together. Stir in the cranberries and orange segments.

Pour the batter by large spoon or pitcher onto a hot greased griddle or frying pan. Turn the pancakes when puffed and bubbling on top. Flip and cook until golden.

Serve with whipped butter and syrup.

Streusel-Topped Squash Bread

Use a smaller, deep-orange heirloom winter squash in this recipe, such as Butternut, Table Queen Acorn, or Delicata.

YIELD: 6 TO 8 SERVINGS

4 tablespoons butter, softened at room temperature

¾ cup packed brown sugar

1 large farmstead egg

½ teaspoon vanilla extract

1 cup cooked, pureed heirloom winter squash

2 cups unbleached all-purpose flour

2 teaspoons baking soda

1 teaspoon cinnamon

½ teaspoon salt

1 cup chopped pecans

TOPPING

½ cup packed dark brown sugar

½ teaspoon cinnamon

½ cup unbleached all-purpose flour

4 tablespoons butter, softened at room temperature

½ cup coarsely chopped pecans

❖ Preheat the oven to 350°F.

Lightly grease and flour a 9 x 5 x 3–inch loaf pan.

Combine the butter and brown sugar in a large bowl, and beat until light and fluffy. Add the egg and vanilla, and mix until blended. Add the squash puree.

Combine the flour, baking soda, cinnamon, and salt in a medium bowl. Stir in the pecans. Use a rubber spatula and gradually fold the flour mixture into the squash mixture just until moistened, and pour into the prepared pan. Spread the topping evenly over the batter.

Bake about 30 minutes or until the edges of the cake begin to pull away from sides of the pan and the topping is brown. Cool completely before cutting.

Serve warm with cream cheese.

TOPPING

Combine the brown sugar, cinnamon, and flour in a small bowl. Cut in the butter with a fork. Stir in the pecans.

HEIRLOOM: DELICATA SQUASH

Introduced in 1894, Delicata squash was popular in the United States until the 1920s. It then disappeared from markets and grocery shelves for several decades. However, in the past few years, this heirloom has experienced renewed interest. Currently found at many supermarkets in the early fall, this variety has regained its wide popularity.

Delicata fruits are small, straight, and oblong, about 7 to

9 inches long, weighing about 2 pounds. The deep orange-yellow flesh is firm and smooth and incredibly sweet. The skin

is thin and cream colored with green and orange stripes and splashes along the ribs. Delicata was once known as Sweet Potato, perhaps because it is similar in taste and texture to sweet potatoes. When cut in half lengthwise, the squash makes two single portions, and its seeds are easily removed—two attributes that have made this variety attractive to modern chefs.

Baked Turkey Salad

This recipe is a great way to use leftover Thanksgiving turkey.

YIELD: 10 TO 12 SERVINGS

6 cups chopped cooked turkey (or chicken)

2 tablespoons lemon juice

¾ cup mayonnaise or more, to taste

1 teaspoon salt

2 cups chopped celery

4 large farmstead eggs, hard-cooked

1 10¾-ounce can low-sodium cream of chicken soup

1 teaspoon grated onion

1 cup grated sharp cheddar cheese

1½ cups crushed potato chips

10 to 12 croissants

❖ Lightly grease a 9 x 13–inch baking dish.

Combine the turkey, lemon juice, mayonnaise, salt, celery, eggs, soup, and grated onion in a large bowl; mix well, and spoon into the prepared baking dish. Sprinkle with the cheese and then the potato chips. Cover and refrigerate the dish overnight.

When ready to use, preheat the oven to 400° and bake, uncovered, 20 to 25 minutes.

Serve warm on croissants.

Pork and Pumpkin Stew over Rice

YIELD: 6 SERVINGS

1 2-pound boneless heritage or grass-fed pork roast, cut into 2-inch cubes

1 tablespoon soy sauce

1 teaspoon salt

1 tablespoon finely chopped ginger

1 tablespoon finely chopped garlic

1 medium yellow onion, chopped

½ teaspoon turmeric

2 tablespoons peanut oil

2 teaspoons dried red pepper flakes

2 cups water, divided

1 pound cubed heirloom pumpkin, such as Small Sugar

Chopped peanuts and fresh cilantro for garnish

❖ Marinate the pork with the soy sauce and salt for 1 hour. Place the pork and marinade, ginger, garlic, onion, turmeric, peanut oil, red pepper flakes, and 1 cup of the water in a large saucepan; mix well. Bring to a boil over medium heat, then reduce the heat and cook, covered, for 40 minutes. Add the remaining water and the pumpkin, and cook 15 minutes or until the pork is tender and most liquid has evaporated.

Serve warm over steamed white rice. Garnish with chopped peanuts and chopped fresh cilantro.

Chicken and Dumplings

This recipe was created by my mother when I was a child, and she has now passed it down to me. I requested this dish every year for my birthday dinner. It is how I've always known chicken and dumplings—thick and creamy with lots of doughy dumplings to go around.

YIELD: 6 TO 8 SERVINGS

1 2½-pound fresh whole chicken

2 large heirloom onions, such as Yellow Globe Danvers

1 cup shredded carrots, divided

2 quarts chicken broth

1 to 2 teaspoons chicken broth paste, to taste

2 10¼-ounce cans cream of chicken soup

3 medium zucchini, sliced and cut in half

1 8-ounce package egg noodles

1 box of Bisquick

❖ Place the chicken in a large stockpot, and cover with water. Add one onion cut in large pieces and ⅓ cup of the shredded carrots. Bring to a boil, then cover and simmer until the chicken is falling off the bones. Remove the chicken from the pot, and allow to cool before removing the meat from the bones. Discard the skin and bones.

Pour the broth through a sieve, and save the liquid. Return the liquid to the pot, and add enough chicken broth to make about 4 quarts. Add the meat. Dice the remaining onion, and add to the pot along with the remaining ⅔ cup shredded carrots.

Remove about a ½ cup of the hot liquid to a large bowl, and dissolve the broth paste in it. (Chicken broth paste is very salty, so be careful not to use too much.) Remove about 2 additional cups of hot liquid and add to this bowl. Add the cream of chicken soup, and stir until there are no lumps. Pour into the pot.

Bring the mixture to a boil, reduce the heat, and simmer for about 15 minutes. Add the zucchini and the egg noodles. Cook the dumplings on top of the pot as directed on the box of Bisquick.

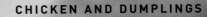

CHICKEN AND DUMPLINGS

GREENS AND SAUSAGE PASTA

Greens and Sausage Pasta

This is an easy, filling, and tasty entrée that you can also make vegetarian by leaving out the sausage. It's a spicy dish so if you're sensitive to hot foods, use a mild sausage and omit the red pepper flakes.

YIELD: 8 TO 10 SERVINGS

¾ pound bow tie pasta

3 tablespoons olive oil, divided

2 cloves garlic, minced

2 tablespoons minced onion

6 andouille sausages, cut into ¼-inch-thick slices

6 cups washed and chopped heirloom chard, collards, and/or kale, such as Red Russian

1 teaspoon salt

1 teaspoon freshly ground black pepper

1 pint ricotta cheese

1 tablespoon hot red pepper flakes

❖ Cook the pasta in a large pot of boiling salted water for about 6 minutes, until al dente. Drain the pasta, and toss with 2 tablespoons of olive oil in a large bowl; set aside.

Heat the remaining tablespoon of olive oil in a large frying pan. Add the garlic and onion, and cook until tender. Add the sausage slices, and cook over medium-high heat until they are browned on both sides. Add the chopped greens, salt, and pepper. Reduce heat to low, and cook, covered, for about 10 minutes or until the greens are soft. Add to the cooked pasta and toss. Add the ricotta cheese and pepper flakes and toss. Serve immediately.

HEIRLOOM: RED RUSSIAN KALE

Kale is a leafy nonheading cabbage and one of the most cold-hardy of vegetables. It grows best in cool weather because its sweet flavor improves after a frost. Americans tend to think of kale as strictly garnish, but it is a tasty, dependable source of vitamins and minerals, containing high amounts of calcium, potassium, and vitamins A and C.

An old variety known in Europe for centuries, Red Russian was brought to Canada by Russian traders. Its flat gray-green leaves have purple leaf stems and veins. In cold weather, the leaves turn completely reddish purple. The leaves of Red Russian kale are exceptionally tender and tasty. For best flavor, they should be eaten immediately after harvesting.

Mexi-Meat Loaf

YIELD: 6 SERVINGS

1 pound ground beef chuck

½ pound ground pork

2 slices day-old bread

⅓ cup canned Mexi-corn, drained (or fresh corn, adding 2 tablespoons chopped red and green bell peppers)

½ cup shredded pepper jack cheese

½ cup chunky salsa, mild or medium, preferably homemade (see page 74)

1 large farmstead egg, beaten

¼ teaspoon red pepper flakes

½ teaspoon cumin

2 tablespoons Worcestershire sauce

❖ Preheat the oven to 350°F.

Mix all the ingredients together with your hands in a large bowl. Spread in an ungreased 9 × 5 × 3–inch loaf pan, and bake in oven for 1½ hours. Remove from oven, and place on a cooling rack for 10 minutes. Turn out meat loaf onto a warmed serving dish.

Garnish with sliced yellow, orange, and red heirloom tomatoes, and serve fresh salsa on the side.

Turkey Soup Provençal

This easy, filling soup is substantial enough for a main course.

YIELD: 4 SERVINGS

1 pound ground turkey breast

½ teaspoon crushed dried herbes de Provence

1 15-ounce can cannelloni beans, drained

1 14.5-ounce can chicken broth

1 14.5-ounce can diced tomatoes with garlic and onion, undrained

4 cups chopped fresh heirloom spinach, such as Bloomsdale Long Standing or King of Denmark

❖ Brown the turkey in a large dutch oven, stirring to crumble. Add the herbs, beans, broth, and tomatoes, and bring to a broil. Reduce the heat and simmer 5 minutes. Stir in the spinach, and simmer 5 minutes longer. Serve immediately.

MEXI-MEAT LOAF

HERB-ROASTED HERITAGE TURKEY

Herb-Roasted Heritage Turkey

YIELD: 8 TO 10 SERVINGS

1 11- to 12-pound heritage turkey

½ cup olive oil

Salt and black pepper, to taste

¾ cup fresh basil leaves

¾ cup fresh thyme leaves and stems

1 apple, quartered

1 red onion, quartered

½ stick butter or margarine, softened

1 teaspoon dried sage

1 teaspoon dried tarragon

1 tablespoon fresh chopped basil

3 cloves garlic, minced

❖ Preheat the oven to 325°F.

Remove the neck and giblets from the turkey. Wash and pat the turkey dry. Rub the inside and outside of the turkey with the olive oil. Salt and pepper the inside of the turkey. Place half of the basil leaves and thyme leaves into the turkey cavity. Add the apple and red onion quarters and the remaining basil and thyme leaves.

Combine the softened butter, sage, tarragon, chopped basil, and minced garlic in a small bowl. Gently loosen the skin on the breast of the turkey, and work the mixture under the skin, spreading out as far as possible. Sprinkle the entire turkey with salt and pepper.

Place the turkey breast side up on a rack in a large roasting pan. Do not cover. Roast the turkey about 3½ hours or until the internal temperature is 175°F. (Use a meat thermometer in the thigh or breast to measure the temperature.) If the turkey is becoming too brown, tent with aluminum foil.

Remove the turkey from the oven, and let stand 20 minutes before carving.

HEIRLOOM: HERITAGE TURKEY

Heritage turkeys are drastically different from those found in the meat department of your local grocery. How? Heritage breeds are raised naturally on pasture and grow more slowly than modern commercial breeds. Heritage breeds are slaughtered at from seven or eight months of age to up to two years old, rather than at three or four months as are the commercial breeds. When it comes to heritage turkeys, older animals are tastier because they have had more time to accumulate amino acids, fats, and nutrients than younger birds have.

In addition, the more exercise a bird gets, the more interesting its taste will be. Birds raised on pasture move around constantly, eating a varied diet of grass, plants, and insects, as opposed to their commercial cousins, which eat an all-grain diet in confinement. As a result, heritage turkeys are healthy, well-rounded birds with a deep, complex flavor and texture that is far superior in quality to any poultry found at the supermarket. Because of this refined flavor, heritage birds do not need to be injected, basted, or even covered when cooked.

Grandma Beach's Marinated Carrots

This salad is delicious and beautiful, with the intense colors of the heirloom vegetables.

YIELD: 8 TO 10 SERVINGS

5 cups heirloom carrots, such as Scarlet Nantes, cut into
¼-inch slices

1 cup sugar

1 teaspoon sea salt

½ cup diced onions (red or yellow)

1 bell pepper, diced

¼ cup white wine vinegar

1 teaspoon prepared mustard

½ teaspoon freshly ground black pepper

½ cup vegetable oil

½ cup condensed tomato soup

1 teaspoon Worcestershire sauce

❖ Place the carrots in a large saucepan, and cover with water. Cook the carrots until just tender, then drain well. Add the sugar and salt to the hot carrots, and mix well. Add the remaining ingredients, and mix well.

Refrigerate overnight in a covered container, stirring occasionally. (This will keep for two weeks in the refrigerator.)

HEIRLOOM:
SCARLET NANTES CARROT

A classic among carrots, the bright reddish orange Scarlet Nantes has old-time carrot flavor. This standard is now widely adapted and has a reputation for sweet flavor and crisp texture. Its cylindrical, blunt-tipped roots are approximately 7 inches long by 1½ inches wide and nearly coreless. Its fine-grained flesh and sweetness make it perfect for juicing. The popular Scarlet Nantes is good all around: fresh eating, cooking, freezing, and storing.

GRANDMA BEACH'S MARINATED CARROTS

APPLE-BACON CHOPPED SALAD

Apple-Bacon Chopped Salad

Use a firm, tart apple variety in this salad, such as the classic Newtown Pippin.

YIELD: 8 SERVINGS

2 heads lettuce, rinsed and chopped

2 small apples, cored and diced into 1/2-inch pieces

1 red grapefruit, peeled and sectioned

1 orange, peeled and sectioned

¼ cup green onions, green portion only, chopped

2 avocados, peeled and sliced

4 thick-cut bacon slices, fried until crispy and chopped into
    ½-inch pieces

VINAIGRETTE

2 tablespoons Dijon mustard

3 tablespoons apple cider vinegar

1 shallot, minced

½ cup extra-virgin olive oil

Sea salt and freshly ground black pepper, to taste

❖ Combine the lettuce, apples, grapefruit, orange, green onions, and half of the vinaigrette in a large bowl, then toss to mix. Divide the salad among salad plates, and garnish with the avocado slices and bacon. Drizzle a little of the remaining vinaigrette over each salad, and serve immediately.

VINAIGRETTE

Whisk together the mustard, vinegar, and shallot in a small bowl. Add the olive oil, and whisk until smooth and blended.

Creamed Onions

YIELD: 4 TO 6 SERVINGS

1 pound peeled pearl onions

4 tablespoons butter

4 tablespoons unbleached all-purpose flour

1 cup heavy or whipping cream

½ cup chicken broth

¼ teaspoon cayenne pepper

½ teaspoon salt

❖ Place the onions in a large saucepan, and just cover with water. Bring to a boil, and cook over medium heat until the onions are fork tender. (Cooking time will vary depending on size of onions.)

Meanwhile, melt the butter in a medium saucepan over medium-low heat, then whisk in the flour. Gradually add the cream and the chicken broth, and cook and stir until smooth, thickened, and bubbly. Stir in the cayenne pepper and salt.

Preheat the oven to 325°F.

Grease a medium-size baking dish, and arrange the cooked onions in it. Pour the white sauce over top. Bake, uncovered, until the sauce is bubbly and beginning to brown on top.

Roasted Beet Salad with Pecans and Goat Cheese

YIELD: 6 TO 8 SERVINGS

6 medium heirloom beets, such as Chioggia, trimmed and
    washed

½ cup pecan halves

2 teaspoons olive oil

⅛ teaspoon salt

½ teaspoon freshly ground black pepper

½ pound stemmed and washed fresh spinach leaves, or
    baby field greens

⅓ cup thinly sliced red onions

3 ounces fresh goat cheese, crumbled

DRESSING

6 tablespoons extra-virgin olive oil

2 tablespoons red wine vinegar

¾ teaspoon salt

¼ teaspoon sugar

Freshly ground black pepper

❖ Preheat the oven to 350°F.

Wrap the beets individually in foil, and place on a rimmed baking sheet. Bake until tender, about 1½ hours. Let cool for 20 minutes, then peel by holding the beet under cold running water and rubbing off the skins. Cut the beets into ½-inch wedges, and place in a large mixing bowl.

In another bowl, combine the pecans with the olive oil, salt, and pepper, mixing well to coat the nuts. Spread the mixture on a baking sheet, and bake until toasted, about 7 to 10 minutes. Set aside to cool.

Prepare the dressing and toss the beets with ⅓ of the dressing. Let beets sit for about 1 hour.

When ready to serve the salad, toss the spinach or greens and the red onion in a large bowl with the remaining ⅔ dressing. Arrange on individual serving plates or on a large platter. Top with the beet mixture, pecans, and goat cheese.

DRESSING

Combine the ingredients in a small bowl and mix well.

HEIRLOOM: CHIOGGIA BEET

Chioggia is an Italian heirloom beet named after a sleepy fishing town near Venice, Italy. The beet is diminutive in size (2 to 2½ inches in diameter) with bright crimson skin. When sliced, it reveals magnificent pink and white concentric rings, making it a beautiful addition to salads. Both the root and the leaves are tasty when cooked, offering a sweet, delicate flavor. Chioggia beets have become quite popular with heirloom gardeners and in American specialty markets.

Roasted Heirloom Vegetable Medley

For a special presentation, choose heirloom potatoes with a variety of colors, such as Purple Peruvian, Bintje (yellow), Early Rose (pink), and Garnet Chili (red).

YIELD: 6 TO 8 SERVINGS

1 pound heirloom potatoes, scrubbed

2 Chioggia beets

3 small red or yellow onions, such as Red Wethersfield or
    Yellow Globe Danvers, quartered (or use 6 pearl onions)

2 Atomic Red carrots

1 Early Yellow Summer Crookneck squash

3 tablespoons olive oil

2 teaspoons garlic powder

½ to 1 teaspoon sea salt

¼ teaspoon black pepper

2 teaspoons dried herb of choice, such as thyme, oregano,
    basil, rosemary, marjoram, or savory

❖ Preheat the oven to 400°F. Line a baking sheet with parchment paper or oil it lightly.

Slice the potatoes, beets, onions, and carrots into ¼-inch slices, and cut the squash into ½-inch slices. Place all the vegetables in a large mixing bowl. Drizzle with olive oil.

Mix the garlic powder, salt, pepper, and herbs in a separate bowl. Add to the vegetables, and stir well until all vegetables are coated with the oil and herb mixture.

Transfer the vegetables to the prepared baking sheet, and spread them out into a single layer. Place in oven on middle rack to roast for 35 to 45 minutes or until tender. Use a butter knife to test doneness. If it slides easily through the vegetables, then they are ready to be served.

Spiced Apple Chutney

YIELD: 2 CUPS

3 cups peeled and finely chopped heirloom apples, such as
    Spitzenburg

1 cup apple juice or cider

2 tablespoons sugar

½ teaspoon salt

¼ teaspoon cinnamon

¼ teaspoon ground coriander

¼ teaspoon freshly grated nutmeg

¼ teaspoon ground ginger or 1 teaspoon fresh ginger

¼ cup golden raisins, plumped in hot water then drained

Salt and freshly ground pepper, to taste

❖ Combine all the ingredients in a medium saucepan. Simmer until the apples are tender. Strain the apples, and return the liquid to the stove. Cook until the juice is reduced by half. Allow the liquid to cool slightly before mixing with the cooked apples. Taste and adjust salt and sugar, if needed.

Cranberry Salad

This recipe has been in my family for years and has been served at every Thanksgiving meal for as long as I can remember. It is an unconventional take on the traditional cranberry salad that will pleasantly surprise you. The cream cheese topping is like frosting on the cake, and the port gives it a little kick that elevates the ingredients. It is delicious served with turkey or simply by itself.

YIELD: 12 TO 16 SERVINGS

1 6-ounce package raspberry Jell-O

1½ cups boiling water

1 20-ounce can crushed pineapple with juice

1 16-ounce can whole cranberry sauce

⅔ cup port

½ cup chopped walnuts

1 8-ounce package cream cheese

4 ounces sour cream

1 cup sliced almonds

❖ Combine the Jell-O and boiling water in a 9 × 13–inch glass baking dish, stirring about 5 minutes or until the Jell-O is completely dissolved. Add the pineapple with juice and the cranberry sauce, wine, and walnuts. Cover and place in the refrigerator for one hour.

Beat the cream cheese until smooth, and stir in the sour cream. Spread on top of the salad. Sprinkle the sliced almonds on top.

Refrigerate for two hours, then slice into squares and serve.

CRANBERRY SALAD

Warm Red Cabbage Salad

This German heritage recipe offers the sweet and tangy combination of a brown sugar and vinegar dressing.

YIELD: 8 SERVINGS

1 head heirloom red cabbage, such as Red Drumhead, chopped coarsely

1 to 2 teaspoons lemon juice or white wine vinegar

1 cup water, divided

4 to 6 slices bacon, cut into ½-inch pieces

2 tablespoons unbleached all-purpose flour

¼ cup firmly packed light brown sugar

¼ cup white wine vinegar

1 large red heirloom onion, such as Southport Red Globe, sliced thinly

¼ teaspoon sea salt

Dash of freshly ground black pepper

❖ Cut up the cabbage and place in a large pot with 1 teaspoon lemon juice or vinegar and ½ cup of the water. Steam cabbage about 10 minutes or until tender. Do not drain. Set the cabbage aside.

Fry the bacon pieces in a cast-iron skillet until browned. Add the flour and brown sugar, and cook over medium heat until bubbly. Add the ¼ cup vinegar, remaining ½ cup water, and onion. Cook until the onion is just tender.

Add the cooked cabbage, salt, and pepper. Coat the cabbage with the brown sugar dressing mixture. Serve warm.

This also can be frozen in containers, then warmed in a pan for use later.

HEIRLOOM:
RED DRUMHEAD CABBAGE

This hardy heirloom dates to the 1860s and is considered the best of all red cabbages because of its fine, remarkably sweet flavor. Its round, slightly flat deep purple heads measure about 7 inches in diameter and are very hardy winter keepers. Red Drumhead is delicious served raw in salads or served cooked or pickled. It holds its color well even when pickled. Red Drumhead has been widely adapted to a range of climates.

Sweet Cabbage Pierogi

YIELD: 12 TO 15 SERVINGS

SWEET CABBAGE FILLING

1 pound heirloom green cabbage, such as Early Jersey Wakefield or Late Flat Dutch, finely chopped

1 teaspoon salt

1 tablespoon butter

1 teaspoon sugar

Salt and pepper, to taste

DOUGH

3 large farmstead eggs

¼ cup water

½ pint sour cream

1 teaspoon salt

4 cups unbleached all-purpose flour

Sweet cabbage filling

❖ **SWEET CABBAGE FILLING**

Add the 1 teaspoon of salt to the cabbage, and let sit for several minutes. Squeeze out the water from the cabbage. Fry the cabbage in the butter, then add the sugar. Fry until golden brown, stirring often. Season to taste, and set aside.

DOUGH

Beat the eggs, water, sour cream, and salt in a large bowl. Gradually add flour, and keep adding until the dough is easy to handle. Knead lightly.

Divide the dough into two portions and cover with a clear kitchen towel. Let rest for 10 to 25 minutes. Roll the dough out thin, and cut rounds with a water glass or round cookie cutter. Place a spoonful of cooled filling in the center, then fold over and pinch ends together well.

Boil a large pot of salted water, and drop the pierogi a few at a time into the boiling water. Boil only until they rise to the top of the water and stay there for a few seconds. Remove with a slotted spoon, and drain in a colander. Rinse lightly with hot water, and then coat with melted butter to prevent sticking.

Serve topped with onions sautéed in butter. Pierogi can be frozen.

Candied Sweet Potatoes

‖♦‖

YIELD: 4 TO 6 SERVINGS

4 heirloom sweet potatoes, such as Southern Queen, peeled
   and quartered

2 cups sugar

¾ cup water

1 teaspoon cinnamon

¼ teaspoon salt

2 tablespoons vinegar

4 tablespoons butter

❖ Preheat the oven to 350°F.

Place potatoes in a large saucepan, cover with water, and bring to a boil. Cook until tender, then drain well. Place the potatoes in a 2-quart baking dish.

In a small saucepan, boil the sugar, water, cinnamon, salt, vinegar, and butter for 5 minutes, stirring constantly. Pour the sauce over the potatoes. Bake 1 hour.

SWEET POTATOES VERSUS YAMS

In the southern United States, where hundreds of varieties of sweet potatoes are grown, many people refer to sweet potatoes as yams, although the two are botanically unrelated. The confusion between sweet potatoes and yams arose from an advertising campaign in the 1940s by Louisiana sweet potato growers who decided that calling their crop Louisiana yams would give it a certain panache. To further confuse Americans, grocers all over the country often label and sell sweet potatoes as yams. Most Americans still incorrectly use the two terms interchangeably.

The sweet potato is a member of the morning glory family (*Convolvulaceae*) and is native to tropical America (Central and South America). Yams are in a family all their own (*Dioscoreaceae*) and are tubers of a tropical vine found in Africa and Asia.

All so-called yams in the United States are actually sweet potatoes, and although the terms are used interchangeably, the U.S. Department of Agriculture requires that the label Yam always be accompanied by the label Sweet Potato. The true yam is not sold or grown commercially anywhere in the United States.

A sweet potato is generally smooth with thin skin; a yam is rough and scaly. Sweet potatoes are moist and sweet; yams are dry and starchy. A sweet potato's skin ranges from creamy white to dark brown; the flesh can be white, yellow, or orange.

Eggplant Parmesan Gratin

YIELD: 6 SERVINGS

1 pound heirloom eggplant, such as Rosa Bianca

3 tablespoons olive oil

1 tablespoon salt

2 large tomatoes, sliced ¼-inch thick

1 small onion, chopped

2 cloves garlic, chopped

1 teaspoon oregano

1 teaspoon basil

½ teaspoon black pepper

½ cup shredded mozzarella cheese

¾ cup fresh breadcrumbs

1 tablespoon butter

❖ Preheat the oven to 425°F.

Lightly grease an 8 × 8–inch baking pan.

Peel several strips of skin from the eggplant, and cut the eggplant into 2-inch cubes. Toss the eggplant with oil, then add the salt and toss to coat.

Spread out the cubes on a lined baking sheet, and place in the oven. Bake 20 to 25 minutes, stirring occasionally until cooked through and browned. Reduce the oven heat to 350°F.

Place half the eggplant in the prepared dish. Arrange the tomato slices on top of the eggplant. Add the chopped onion and garlic, and sprinkle with the herbs; pepper; and a little salt, if needed. Cover the tomatoes with the remaining eggplant, followed by the cheese; sprinkle with breadcrumbs and dot with butter.

Bake 20 minutes or until the cheese is melted and the breadcrumbs are golden brown.

HEIRLOOM: ROSA BIANCA EGGPLANT

Until the early twentieth century, Americans grew eggplants strictly as ornamentals, with many varieties displaying delicate flowers and attractive foliage as part of a border or a bed. There is a whole array of interesting and beautiful eggplant varieties other than the typical purple-black ones found at the grocery: long and skinny green (Thai Long Green), white (White), orange (Turkish Orange), and purple streaked (Listada de Gandia), all with intricate tastes and textures.

Rosa Bianca is a beautiful Italian heirloom eggplant. Its teardrop-shaped and pink-lavender fruits grow 4 to 6 inches long and have tender, creamy, mild-flavored flesh without bitterness. Rosa Bianca is a popular eggplant among chefs and gardeners, and some growers consider it the best variety of eggplant. The fruits from the Rosa Bianca eggplant are so beautiful that they can easily become the centerpiece on a table.

Pumpkin Pie

I experimented and combined a few different recipes to get the consistency and spices just right for this Thanksgiving Day favorite.

⫚

YIELD: 8 SERVINGS

1 pie pumpkin, such as Seminole or Winter Luxury

1 cup firmly packed light brown sugar

2 tablespoons unbleached all-purpose flour

½ teaspoon salt

3 to 4 teaspoons pumpkin pie spice

2 large eggs

1⅔ cups evaporated milk

1 9-inch deep-dish piecrust shell (frozen and unbaked, or your own homemade crust)

❖ Preheat the oven to 375°F.

Cut the pumpkin in half, and remove the seeds. Roast the pumpkin in a glass dish covered with foil for about 1 hour. When cool, remove pumpkin from skin and mash. Reserve 1½ cups.

Preheat the oven to 450°F.

Mix the brown sugar, flour, salt, and pumpkin pie spice in a large bowl. Stir in the eggs. Beat in the pumpkin and the evaporated milk until smooth, then pour into the piecrust.

Bake for 15 minutes, then reduce the heat to 325°F, and bake an additional 45 minutes or until a knife inserted comes out clean.

HEIRLOOM:
SEMINOLE PUMPKIN

The origin of the Seminole pumpkin can be traced back to the 1500s, when early explorers found it growing wild in the Florida Everglades. The native Seminole Indians cultivated this pumpkin by planting the seeds at the base of dead trees, where the vines could grow up the trunk and the fruit could hang from the bare limbs.

Although the Seminole pumpkin was introduced commercially in 1916, it is rarely grown today. However, it is poised for a revival in its native Florida thanks to its tolerance of hot and humid conditions and resistance to pests. Pear shaped or spherical and small at 6 to 8 inches wide, the pump-kins have a buff-colored shell that is so hard it must be split with an ax. Inside, the flesh is beige and sweet. Its flavor is legendary and simply cannot be beat—excellent for pie filling or any recipe calling for pumpkin. In addition to its culinary uses, the Seminole pumpkin makes a gorgeous seasonal decoration.

PUMPKIN PIE

Spitzenburg Apple Pie

❦❦❦

YIELD: 8 SERVINGS

CRUST

1 cup unbleached all-purpose flour

1 cup whole wheat flour

Pinch of salt

10 tablespoons cold butter

1 large farmstead egg

APPLE FILLING

2½ pounds Spitzenburg apples

⅓ cup honey or less, to taste

2 tablespoons fresh lemon juice

1 teaspoon cinnamon

½ teaspoon nutmeg

1 tablespoon unbleached all-purpose flour

❖ **CRUST**

Combine the flours and salt in a large bowl. Cut in the butter with a pastry blender until uniformly blended. Moisten the dough with the egg, form into a disk, wrap in plastic wrap, and chill while you prepare the apple filling.

APPLE FILLING

Core and slice the apples (peeling is optional) and place in a large bowl. Add the honey, lemon juice, cinnamon, nutmeg, and flour, and toss to mix. Set aside.

Preheat the oven to 400°F.

Cut the pastry dough in half, and roll out on a floured surface. Use tablespoons of ice water to moisten as needed. Line a 9-inch pie plate with the pastry. Put filling on top of pastry. Roll out the other half of the dough for the top of the pie. Slide onto the pie, and flute the edges to seal. Cut a few vents in the top crust.

Bake 10 minutes, then reduce the heat to 350°F. Continue baking 35 to 40 minutes or until the apples are fork tender. If desired, serve with vanilla ice cream or honey.

HEIRLOOM: ESOPUS SPITZENBURG APPLE

Said to be one of Thomas Jefferson's favorite apple varieties, the Esopus Spitzenburg was discovered in the early 1700s at Esopus, New York, most likely by a Dutch settler named Spitzenburg. Jefferson wasn't the only passionate consumer of the Spitzenburg apple. A. J. Downing, America's foremost nineteenth-century pomologist, described it as "a handsome, truly delicious apple . . . unsurpassed as a dessert fruit . . . considered the first of apples."

The handsome red–orange apples with their firm, juicy, yellow flesh have an unforgettably rich spicy and aromatic flavor. Modern apple connoisseurs still consider the Spitzenburg to be one of the finest varieties in existence.

Persimmon Pudding

This "pudding" is a cross between fudge and a fallen cake.

❚❙❚

YIELD: 18 SERVINGS

2 cups persimmon pulp

2 cups sugar

2 large farmstead eggs, lightly beaten

1 teaspoon baking soda

1½ cups buttermilk

1½ cups unbleached all-purpose flour

1 teaspoon baking powder

½ teaspoon ground cinnamon

⅛ teaspoon salt

¼ cup heavy cream

1 teaspoon vanilla

4 tablespoons butter

❖ Preheat the oven to 325°F.

In a large bowl, combine the pulp, sugar, and eggs. In a measuring cup, mix the baking soda into the buttermilk stirring until the foaming stops. Add the buttermilk mixture to the pulp mixture, and mix well.

Sift the flour, baking powder, cinnamon, and salt together in a small bowl, and add to the pulp mixture, beating well. Add the cream and vanilla, and mix well.

Melt the butter in a 9 × 13–inch baking pan. Pour the melted butter into the batter, leaving just enough butter in the pan to grease the bottom. Mix the batter and the butter.

Pour the batter into the prepared pan, and bake 45 minutes or until set. Serve warm or cooled with whipped cream.

THE PERSIMMON

The word *persimmon* comes from an Algonquin word meaning "a dry fruit." The ancient tree is native to Burma, China, India, and Japan. Chronicles of the persimmon date to the fourteenth century, when Marco Polo recorded a trade in persimmons with the Chinese. Seeds were first introduced to the United States in 1856, sent from Japan by Commodore Matthew Perry. The U.S. Department of Agriculture imported grafted trees in 1870 and distributed them to California and the southern states, where they were found to be best adapted.

Although there are thousands of varieties of persimmons grown in China and Japan, only two are commercially available in the United States. The Hachiya variety makes up about 90 percent of the fruit sold in the United States. It is has an acornlike shape and is tart until it becomes soft ripe. The Fuyu variety is gaining popularity in the United States and is similar in color to the Hachiya, but it looks more like a squashed tomato. It is smaller, sweeter, and edible while still firm.

Persimmons can be found in most supermarkets during the fall, but there is not a large demand outside ethnic markets. Choose persimmons with deep red undertones. Look for persimmons that are round and plump with a glossy, smooth skin. Avoid fruits with blemishes, bruises, or cracked skin and missing the green leaves at the top.

The American Persimmon (*Diospyros virginiana*) is a native American tree that grows 30 to 45 feet tall. Its lustrous green leaves and rough brown bark produce beautiful yellow to orange golf ball–size fruit that remains on the trees after the leaves fall. The drooping branches give this tree a graceful appearance. Edible persimmon fruits (1 to 2 inches around) mature in fall to an orange to reddish purple color and may persist on the tree into winter. Persimmon fruit is quite astringent when green, but upon ripening it becomes sweet and smooth-textured and may be eaten off the tree. Pick fruit while it is firm yet fully colored, and allow it to soften and finish ripening indoors.

BAKED APPLES

Baked Apples

—— ¶|¶ ——

6 large baking apples, such as Calville Blanc d'Hiver

1 tablespoon butter

6 tablespoons sugar

1 teaspoon cinnamon

½ cup water

½ cup corn syrup

Cream (optional)

❖ Preheat the oven to 350°F.

Wash and pare the apples halfway down from the stem end. Remove the cores, leaving the apples whole. Place the apples in a flat baking dish.

Mix the sugar and cinnamon in a small bowl. In the center of each apple, place ½ teaspoon of the butter and 1 tablespoon of the sugar-cinnamon mixture. Combine the water and corn syrup in a small bowl, and pour over the apples.

Bake 45 minutes. Baste occasionally with the juices to glaze the apples.

Serve with cream on the side, if desired.

HEIRLOOM:
CALVILLE BLANC D'HIVER APPLE

Although the definitive origin of the Calville Blanc d'Hiver apple is unknown, it can be traced back to Normandy, France, where it was planted in the early 1600s. It has become known as the classic French dessert apple for its tart and juicy taste and its ability to maintain its shape when cooked.

Green and misshapen when harvested in October, the Calville Blanc turns yellow and develops maximum flavor with maturity—at least one month after picking. Its ugly exterior masks a sublime interior, and its distinctive flavor has been described by some as effervescent.

Pumpkin Spice Bundt Cake

❖❖❖

YIELD: 8 TO 10 SERVINGS

2 cups unbleached all-purpose flour

2 teaspoons baking powder

1 teaspoon baking soda

1 teaspoon cinnamon

1 teaspoon nutmeg

½ teaspoon ground ginger

1 tablespoon orange zest

2 cups cooked, pureed heirloom pumpkin, such as Winter Luxury

½ cup sour cream

½ cup sugar

1 cup packed light brown sugar

½ cup milk

¼ cup butter

2 large farmstead eggs

2 tablespoons butter

1 cup spiced dark rum

Whipped cream

❖ Preheat the oven to 350°F.

Combine the flour, baking powder, baking soda, cinnamon, nutmeg, ginger, and orange zest in a large bowl. Add the pumpkin, sour cream, sugar, brown sugar, milk, and ¼ cup butter. Beat until well combined. Add the eggs and beat for two minutes.

Pour into a nonstick Bundt pan, and bake for 45 to 50 minutes or until a toothpick inserted in the middle comes out clean. Cool completely, then overturn onto a serving plate.

Combine the remaining 2 tablespoons butter and the rum in a saucepan, and simmer for a few minutes. Slowly pour the rum mixture over the cake, allowing it to soak as you go. Serve immediately with a dollop of freshly whipped cream. Refrigerate leftovers.

PUMPKIN SPICE BUNDT CAKE

WINTER

 Winter marks the end of the farmer's year, when the weather won't allow anyone to grow much. Snow blankets the fields, and plants enter their dormant period. Farmers can still harvest cold-hardy plants such as cabbage and kale, but for the most part we rely on our steadfast summer and fall preparations to get us through the season. However, a bit of outdoor pruning can still be done.

The cold months are the time to catch up on record-keeping, planning, reading, and researching plants and equipment for next year's growing season. It is also the time when we can travel or work on indoor projects such as home maintenance and remodeling, including leisurely pursuits such as spinning, knitting, and quilting.

The winter holidays bring an abundance of family and friends together, so our hobby-farm kitchens are busy as usual, preparing seasonal delights for gatherings and gifts. For holiday treats, we look to our stored squashes, root vegetables, and apples to liven up the dinner table and, of course, to our succulent roasted meats harvested from the farm.

TOWNLINE FARM
HEIRLOOM GROWER ## POULTRY RESERVE

*H*eirlooms, in the context of this book, do not mean just fruits and vegetables. For Bill and Dayna Yockey, heritage breeds of poultry are also thought to be national culinary treasures. In 1991, after learning about the American Livestock Breeds Conservancy's efforts to preserve historic breeds of livestock and poultry, Bill redirected his farming focus from sheep and commercial turkeys to the preservation of rare poultry breeds. Townline Sheep Farm became Townline Farm Poultry Reserve, and the first heritage turkeys, twelve Midget White poults, arrived shortly after. Next came Wishard Bronze and Kardosh Bronze poults, and within two years the farm supported twenty-five breeding pairs. Before long, Bill was raising nine different breeds. He has since scaled back to two because, in his words, "you can't save them all."

Situated in Crawford County in northwestern Pennsylvania, Townline Farm Poultry Reserve lies in the Lakeland region, with Lake Erie to the north and a host of smaller lakes just a few miles away. The land is relatively flat but robust with sugar maples, oaks, walnuts, and hickory trees among the woods, wetlands, and traditional farms of the region. The Yockeys' farm happens to be located in the eastern flyway for migratory waterfowl, and the surrounding lakes are stopover points. Birds are familiar sights in these parts, as are their natural predators—raccoons, red foxes, coyotes, owls, herons, hawks, and the occasional black bear. Townline Farm's domestic birds are protected by six guard donkeys and an electric fence, which has kept down the number of predator kills.

Farming is a part-time endeavor for the Yockeys, as Bill and Dayna both work off-site—Bill as a licensed clinical social worker and notary public, and Dayna as a registered nurse. Yet they still run a steady business selling birds and eggs to local consumers and through their Web site. Their flock of rare turkeys (Kardosh Bronze and Midget White), chickens (Dark Cornish and Buckeyes), and geese (American Buff and Pilgrim) are naturally bred, hatched, and sustainably pasture grazed. They do not employ "chicken tractor" confinement, preferring that the birds be truly free to roam in large pastures. No feed additives or hormones are ever used on the flock, and all of Townline Farm's turkey feed is locally grown and ground to order. The Yockeys offer hatching eggs, poults, and goslings; brown eggs for eating (as opposed to hatching); and finished table birds (turkey, chicken, and poussin) for fine dining.

In addition to their support for rare and endangered poultry breeds, Bill and Dayna enthusiastically support the "buy fresh, buy local" movement, so they purchase pastured pork from a neighbor and cook daily with fresh, locally grown ingredients. They also grow a kitchen garden of vegetables and herbs and eat plenty of their own chickens and turkeys through-

out the year. With dedication and passion, the Yockeys are helping to sustain American heritage breeds, and they are transforming Thanksgiving tables everywhere in the process.

Townline Farm Poultry Reserve
14563 Townline Road
Linesville, PA 16424
(877) 632-9242
http://www.townlinefarm.com

RADISH SALSA

Radish Salsa

YIELD: 2 CUPS

½ large shallot or red onion

1 teaspoon salt

¼ cup rice wine or white vinegar

1 lemon (for juice and zest)

1½ cups finely diced heirloom radish, such as French Breakfast

1 jalapeño, minced with or without seeds (depending on desired heat)

1 clove garlic, minced

1 tablespoon olive oil

2 teaspoons dried cilantro

Salt and freshly ground pepper, to taste

❖ Finely chop the shallot and place in a medium bowl. Add the 1 teaspoon salt, and cover with the vinegar and lemon juice. Allow to stand for 20 minutes at room temperature. Strain the shallot, reserving the liquid. Add the radish, jalapeño, and garlic to the shallot. Stir in the olive oil. Add the lemon zest and cilantro, and then season with salt and pepper. Add as much of the reserved vinegar as desired. Let the mixture stand for at least 30 minutes before serving with sesame crackers.

HEIRLOOM: FRENCH BREAKFAST RADISH

Radishes grow quickly, especially in cool weather, so they are planted in spring and in fall. French Breakfast is a short season radish (it grows in just twenty-three days) that dates to 1879 Europe. It is widely grown today by heirloom enthusiasts. French Breakfast is a charming, blunt-tipped, 2-inch-long radish with rosy scarlet coloring that fades to a white tip. Its flesh is white and crisp with a mildly pungent but pleasing taste. The roots and tops can be pickled or cooked.

Onion Tart with Havarti

For a finger food appetizer, cut this rich tart into small squares. For a side dish to a green salad or a bowl of soup, cut this into wedges.

🍴

YIELD: 8 SIDE DISH SERVINGS OR 16 APPETIZER SERVINGS

DOUGH

2¾ cups unbleached all-purpose flour
1/4 teaspoon salt
1 large farmstead egg, beaten
1½ tablespoons olive oil
6 tablespoons butter, melted and cooled
⅓ cup cold milk

FILLING

3 tablespoons olive oil
6 cups thinly sliced yellow heirloom onions, such as Ailsa
   Craig Exhibition
Salt and pepper, to taste
1 large farmstead egg, beaten
8 ounces Havarti cheese, cut into small chunks
1 cup grated Emmentaler or Gruyere cheese

❖DOUGH

In a large bowl, stir together the flour and salt. Make a well in the center, and add the egg, 1½ tablespoons of the oil, the melted butter, and the milk to the well. Working in the center of the well, mix together the liquid ingredients, gradually incorporating flour until a dough forms.

Turn the dough out onto a floured surface, and knead until smooth, about 10 minutes. Form the dough into a ball, wrap in a kitchen towel, and let stand at room temperature for 2 hours.

FILLING

In a large nonstick skillet, cook the onions in the olive oil over medium-low heat until tender but not brown, stirring frequently. (This step may take up to 45 minutes. Cooking the onions slowly brings out their full sweetness.) Season the onions with salt and pepper, and cool to room temperature. Mix in the egg, then the Havarti cheese.

Preheat the oven to 375°F.

On a floured surface, roll out the dough to form a 13-inch round. Transfer to a baking sheet, and fold outer inch of dough over to form a rim. Bake the crust for 10 minutes.

Remove the baking sheet from the oven, and spread the onion topping evenly over the crust; then sprinkle with Emmentaler or Gruyere cheese. Bake until the crust is golden, about 15 to 20 minutes longer. Remove the tart to a large cutting board. Let cool slightly before cutting.

HEIRLOOM:
AILSA CRAIG EXHIBITION ONION

This large yellow Spanish-type onion was introduced in the United States in 1887 by David Murray, gardener for the Marquess of Ailsa. The onion was named after the most conspicuous landmark in the channel between Ireland and Scotland—the Scottish island of Ailsa Craig—a small, round, solid land mass resembling a curling stone. British gardeners grew this almost perfectly round onion for garden shows because its yellow-skinned bulbs grow very large (3 pounds or more, with the average being 2 pounds), and its white sweet flesh is mild and tasty. The Ailsa Craig Exhibition onion is considered a cross between the Yellow Globe Danvers and the Cranston's Excelsior.

ONION TART WITH HAVARTI

Balsamic Roasted Garlic

Put a spoonful of this delicious spread in your favorite soup, or spread it on fresh Italian flat bread before baking.

SERVES 6 TO 8

½ cup good-quality balsamic vinegar

½ cup extra-virgin olive oil

1 tablespoon whole or ground dried rosemary, or to taste

6 to 8 bulbs heirloom hardneck garlic, such as Spanish Roja (tops cut off about ¼ inch)

❖ Combine the balsamic vinegar, olive oil, and rosemary in a foil-lined shallow baking dish or pan. Add the garlic, cut side down, and wrap the foil around the garlic to seal it in. Set aside to marinate at least 1 to 2 hours or overnight.

Preheat the oven to 375°F.

Place the baking dish on the center rack of the oven. Bake 40 to 50 minutes. Remove the garlic from the oven and let cool. The garlic should pop right out of the skins. Mash with a fork.

Spread on bread or add to sauces. The garlic can also be placed in a food processor with ½ cup olive oil and a pinch of salt to make a paste to add to soup or spread on crusty bread.

Roasted Garlic on Party Rye

Use a hardneck heirloom variety such as Chesnok Red, Music, or Georgian Crystal for a true garlic aroma and flavor that stands up well in recipes.

SERVES 15 TO 20

1 bulb heirloom garlic

Olive oil

Salt, pepper, thyme, or rosemary, to taste

1 loaf party rye bread

Smoked salmon or cooked shrimp

❖ Preheat the oven to 350°F.

Slice off the top off the garlic bulb, allowing the cloves to be exposed. Drizzle with olive oil, and sprinkle with desired seasonings.

Place the garlic bulbs in a shallow baking dish, and cover with foil. Bake 45 minutes or until the cloves are soft. Remove the baking dish from the oven, and allow the garlic to cool.

Squeeze the soft garlic cloves into a small bowl. Spread the roasted garlic over the party rye bread and top with smoked salmon or cooked shrimp.

Sweet Potato Soup

This appetizer pairs well with a seafood entrée or baked poultry.

YIELD: 4 SERVINGS

3 to 4 medium-size heirloom sweet potatoes, such as Nancy Hall

1 cup diced sweet heirloom onion, such as Walla Walla or Yellow Sweet Spanish

2 tablespoons butter

4 cups chicken stock

1 green bell pepper, seeded and finely diced

Salt, to taste

¼ cup finely chopped sun-dried tomato

Lime cream

LIME CREAM

½ cup sour cream

Juice of 1 lime

1 tablespoon lime zest

❖ Cook the sweet potatoes in a large pot of salted water until tender, then drain, cool, and peel. Sauté the onion in the butter in a heavy saucepan. Puree the potatoes, onion, and 1 cup of the chicken stock in a food processor. Place in the saucepan with the remaining stock. Add the green pepper and salt. Simmer covered for 30 minutes.

Sprinkle the sun-dried tomato over the soup, and drizzle with lime cream before serving.

LIME CREAM

Combine the ingredients in a small bowl. Chill until ready to serve the soup.

Curried Squash Soup

YIELD: 6 TO 8 SERVINGS

4 tablespoons butter

3 tablespoons curry powder

Freshly ground black pepper, to taste

1 pound finely chopped yellow onions

5 tablespoons coarsely chopped garlic

3 tablespoons coarsely chopped fresh ginger

4 cups cooked orange heirloom winter squash, such as
   Butternut or Delicata

4 cups chicken stock

1 cup coconut milk

1 cup milk

Salt and white pepper, to taste

Sour cream or plain yogurt and roasted squash seeds, for
   garnish

❖ Preheat the oven to 400 °F.

Cut the squash in half and scoop out seeds and seedbed. Place cut side up on an oven rack, and bake until soft, about 20 to 40 minutes (less for a smaller squash, more for a larger one). Let cool, and scrape flesh from rind.

Melt the butter in a large frying pan over medium heat, and add the curry powder and black pepper. Heat, stirring constantly for 1 minute. Add the onion, garlic, and ginger, and sauté until onion is tender. Remove from heat and cool slightly.

Working in batches, puree the squash, onion mixture, and chicken stock in a blender until smooth. Pour into a large stockpot, and bring to a simmer. Stir in the coconut milk and milk, and heat through (do not allow the soup to boil). Add salt and white pepper to taste.

Serve in individual bowls topped with a dollop of sour cream or yogurt, and sprinkle with roasted seeds.

ROASTING PUMPKIN OR SQUASH SEEDS
Preheat the oven to 400 °F.

Remove all flesh from the seeds, then rinse and drain well. Put seeds in a bowl, and drizzle with enough vegetable oil to coat well. Roast the seeds in a shallow pan, stirring frequently until the seeds are golden brown and crispy. Drain on paper towels, and sprinkle with salt.

Spicy Pumpkin Bread

YIELD: 12 TO 15 SERVINGS

3¼ cups unbleached all-purpose flour

1 teaspoon baking powder

1 teaspoon baking soda

1 teaspoon cloves

1 teaspoon nutmeg

2 teaspoons salt

1 teaspoon cinnamon

2 cups cooked heirloom pumpkin, such as Small Sugar

1 cup vegetable oil

3 cups sugar

4 large farmstead eggs

❖ Preheat the oven to 350°F.

Lightly grease and flour two loaf pans.

Sift together the flour, baking powder, baking soda, cloves, nutmeg, salt, and cinnamon in a large bowl. Combine the pumpkin, oil, sugar, and eggs in a medium bowl, and mix well. Stir the pumpkin mixture into the flour mixture, stirring just until mixed.

Pour the batter into the prepared pans, filling two-thirds full. Bake 1 hour or until a wooden pick placed in the center comes out clean. Cool in pans.

Cranberry Pineapple Scones

YIELD: 4 SERVINGS

½ cup dried cranberries

2 tablespoons Grand Marnier liqueur or orange juice

½ cup chopped pineapple, fresh or canned, in its own juice

1 cup unbleached all-purpose flour

1½ teaspoons baking powder

2 tablespoons sugar

¼ teaspoon kosher salt

3 tablespoons unsalted butter, cut into small cubes

1 large farmstead egg yolk, beaten

¼ cup cream, divided

❖ Preheat the oven to 400°F.

Combine the cranberries and Grand Marnier in a microwavable container, and heat on high for 1 minute or until the cranberries are tender.

Combine the flour, baking powder, sugar, and salt in a medium bowl. Cut in the butter until the mixture is crumbly. Stir in the egg yolk and 2 tablespoons of the cream. Stir in the cranberries and any remaining liquid and pineapple. Add the remaining cream.

Turn dough out onto floured board, and gently knead 10 times. Form a ½-inch-thick rectangle, and cut into four scones, or cut on the diagonal so you have eight smaller scones.

Place the scones on an ungreased baking sheet, and bake about 15 minutes or until golden brown. Set aside to cool slightly before serving.

THE NATIVE CRANBERRY

One of only three fruits native to North America (the other two being Concord grapes and blueberries), the cranberry has played several significant roles there. Long before the pilgrims arrived, native peoples not only ate cranberries but also used them for medicinal and ceremonial purposes. Pilgrims used cranberries to make dyes and poultices, and cranberries were a vital source of vitamin C.

The first commercial cranberry beds were planted in Dennis, Massachusetts, in 1816, by Henry Hall, a Revolutionary War veteran. From that modest beginning, cranberry farming has grown to encompass some 40,000 acres across the northern United States and Canada.

Cranberries are a low-growing, vining, woody perennial plant. Most of them are harvested between September and October, utilizing either the wet or dry harvesting method. In the wet, or water, method (which most people employ), farmers flood the beds; then, using specialized harvesting equipment, they beat the fruit off the vine. They net the floating fruit and load it onto trucks. In dry harvesting, farmers comb the cranberries from the vines using a mechanized picking machine. They then load the fruit into bins and ship it. Wet-harvested cranberries are used to make juice and sauce. Dry-harvested cranberries are packaged as fresh fruit.

Fresh cranberries are available in stores from mid-September through December. Take advantage of their fresh availability, and freeze in abundance. To freeze cranberries, double wrap them in plastic without washing the fruit. To use frozen cranberries, just rinse them in cold water—no thawing is necessary. In fact, best results are obtained without thawing.

Apple Crepes

This dish makes a wonderful winter brunch.

YIELD: 4 SERVINGS

3 cooking apples, such as Calville Blanc d'Hiver

¼ cup plus 6 tablespoons butter, divided

3 tablespoons sugar, divided

1 teaspoon cinnamon

4 large farmstead eggs

⅓ cup milk

½ cup unbleached all-purpose flour

½ teaspoon salt

Confectioners' sugar

❖ Pare and thinly slice the apples.

Heat ¼ cup of butter in a 10-inch skillet, and add the apple slices. Cover and cook over medium heat until the apples are almost tender.

Combine 2 tablespoons of the sugar and the cinnamon in a small bowl. Sprinkle evenly over the apples. Cook until the apples are tender, then set aside and keep warm.

Beat the eggs in a medium bowl until thick. Stir in the milk. Add the flour, the remaining tablespoon of sugar, and the salt. Beat the mixture until there are no more lumps.

Heat 3 tablespoons of the butter in a large skillet until moderately hot. Drop ¼ cup of batter into the skillet. Turn the pan from side to side to coat the entire pan evenly with batter. Spoon some of the apple mixture on top of the batter, then cover with additional batter. Cook until brown on the bottom. Turn and brown on the other side.

Remove to a platter, brush with some of the remaining butter, and sprinkle with confectioners' sugar. Keep warm.

Repeat the procedure with the remaining batter and apples.

Maple Pumpkin Muffins

YIELD: 1 DOZEN

2 cups unbleached all-purpose flour

¾ cup plus 2 tablespoons packed dark or golden brown sugar, divided

1 teaspoon pumpkin pie spices

2 teaspoons baking powder

½ teaspoon baking soda

¼ teaspoon salt

2 large farmstead eggs

1 cup canned pumpkin or fresh pumpkin puree

¾ cup evaporated whole milk

¼ cup corn oil

1 teaspoon pure vanilla extract

3 tablespoons pure maple syrup, as dark as possible

½ cup roasted walnuts, chopped

1 3-ounce package softened cream cheese

TOPPING

¼ cup roasted walnuts, chopped

2 tablespoons light brown sugar

❖ Preheat the oven to 400°F.

Combine the flour, ¾ cup of the golden brown sugar, and the spices in a small bowl. Set aside.

In a large bowl, whisk together the eggs, pumpkin puree, milk, oil, vanilla extract, and 1 tablespoon of the maple syrup. Add the dry ingredients, mix just until moistened, and then fold in the nuts.

In a small bowl, beat the cream cheese with the remaining brown sugar and maple syrup. Swirl gently into the batter. Fill the muffin papers ¾ full. Combine walnuts and brown sugar, and sprinkle on top.

Bake for 20 to 25 minutes or until lightly browned and a wooden pick comes out clean when inserted in the center of a muffin.

Yeast Bread with Heirloom Garlic

YIELD: 6 TO 8 SERVINGS

1½ teaspoons dry yeast

1½ cups water, plus 1 or 2 tablespoons more, as needed

15 cloves heirloom garlic, such as Chesnok Red, peeled and crushed

1½ teaspoons salt

2 cups unbleached all-purpose flour

1½ cups whole wheat flour

❖ Dissolve the yeast in water in a large bowl. Stir in the garlic, salt, and flours. Knead the dough until well blended. Oil a medium bowl, add the dough, cover tightly with plastic wrap, and allow to rise 1 hour or until doubled in size.

Punch down the dough, and form into a loaf, either round or elongated. Allow the loaf to rise for 1 hour on a parchment-lined baking sheet. Cover with plastic wrap or a damp towel during the rise.

Preheat the oven to 375°F.

Slash the top of the loaf with a sharp knife. Bake 40 to 45 minutes or until the loaf sounds hollow when tapped and is nicely browned.

Serve with pasta or savory soup or stew.

Pork Roast with Sauerkraut

The sauerkraut in this dish marinates the meat to flavorful tenderness, and the pork sweetens the kraut. If you can find heritage pork, such as Berkshire or Tamworth, in your area, its superior flavor will enhance this dish.

YIELD: SERVES 6 TO 8

3 tablespoons vegetable oil

1 3- to 4-pound fresh heritage pork roast

1 quart homemade sauerkraut (see recipe on page 210)

1 teaspoon salt

½ teaspoon black pepper

❖ Heat a large frying pan, and add the oil. Gently brown the pork roast on all sides in the oil. Place the roast in a large slow cooker. Add the sauerkraut and juice, and tuck around the meat. Add the salt and pepper.

Cover and cook on high for 4 hours or until a meat thermometer inserted at the center of the roast registers between 160°F and 170°F. The meat will easily come apart with a fork and be very tender. (This can also be cooked in a 350°F oven for 1 to 1½ hours or until the meat is tender and registers between 160°F and 170°F.)

Carefully remove the roast with tongs, and place on a serving plate. Spoon the sauerkraut around the roast.

HEIRLOOM: HERITAGE PORK

Today, large vertical corporations produce most of the pork sold in the United States. There was a time not too long ago, however, when farmers and homesteaders always kept a few pigs—breeds we identify today as heritage—for meat and lard. These breeds were naturally thrifty and hardy. They lived off the land, eating pasture grass, grains, fruits, vegetables, and the occasional scraps from the table and whey from the churn. Because heritage breeds do not perform well in the type of confinement operations that are common today, some of the older breeds, such as the Red Wattle and the Large Black, are in danger of extinction.

It is dangerous for any country to have only a handful of modern commercial breeds with the same traits, weakened by excessive inbreeding, as we do today. An epidemic could quickly eradicate them, and without enough variation in the gene pool, we would not have the ability to recover them. Fortunately, an increasing

number of dedicated U.S. farmers are raising heritage breeds, whose genes are being used to improve many modern breeds.

Conservation of heritage breeds requires consuming them, thereby creating demand for their premium meat. Grass-fed heritage pork is firmer and juicier than grain-fed pork, with a sweet and nutty flavor. Lean breeds that have gained a gourmet following for their superior flavor include the Berkshire and the Tamworth. Other heritage breeds include the Gloucester Old Spots, the Hereford, the Mulefoot, and the Red Wattle Hog.

Stuffed Cabbage Rolls

YIELD: 6 TO 8 SERVINGS

½ cup chopped parsley

¼ cup chopped mint

1 teaspoon chopped thyme

2 cloves garlic, crushed

1 medium onion, grated

1 pound ground beef

½ pound ground pork

1½ cups cooked rice

Salt and pepper, to taste

Dash of nutmeg

1 large head green heirloom cabbage, such as Early Jersey
   Wakefield

1 10¾-ounce can tomato soup

½ teaspoon sugar

HEIRLOOM:
EARLY JERSEY WAKEFIELD CABBAGE

This heirloom cabbage variety, also known as True American, has remained a dominant variety for the American home garden since the 1840s. It originated in England in the late 1700s and was first grown in America by Mr. Francis Brill of Jersey City, New Jersey. It's a small compact plant that's 2 to 4 pounds in size, with a pale green conical head and a delicious, mild, sweet flavor. It produces few outer leaves, and its young leaves can be used in salads.

❖ Combine the parsley, mint, thyme, garlic, onion, ground beef, ground pork, rice, salt, pepper, and nutmeg in a large bowl, and mix well.

Remove the core from the cabbage, and place the cabbage in a large stockpot of boiling salted water. Remove leaves as they become tender—just tender enough that they can be rolled without cracking.

Take one leaf at a time, and cut off the heavy core. Place about 2 tablespoons of meat and rice filling at the bottom of the leaf. Roll once, then fold in the sides. Continue rolling to the end of the leaf, and secure with a toothpick. Continue rolling leaves until all the filling has been used. Layer the rolls in a large baking dish.

Preheat the oven to 350°F.

Combine the tomato soup, two cans of water, the sugar, and salt and pepper to taste in a medium bowl, and mix well. Pour the soup mixture over the cabbage rolls. Cover and bake for 1¼ hours.

Turkey Pie

This recipe, as well as the turkey divan casserole that follows, is another great way to use leftover turkey.

YIELD: 6 SERVINGS

1 10-ounce package frozen mixed vegetables

½ cup chopped onion

½ cup chopped mushrooms

¼ cup butter

⅓ cup unbleached all-purpose flour

½ teaspoon salt

¼ teaspoon black pepper

½ teaspoon dried sage

2 cups turkey broth

¾ cup milk

3 cups chopped turkey

½ cup diced parboiled potato

2 10-inch frozen piecrusts, thawed

¼ cup fresh parsley

❖ Preheat the oven to 450°F.

Cook the frozen vegetables according to the package directions, drain, and set aside.

Brown the onions and mushrooms in the butter in a large skillet until tender. Stir in the flour, salt, pepper, and sage. Add the turkey broth and milk, and mix well. Stir in the turkey, potato, and mixed vegetables, and mix well. Cook until thick and bubbly.

Pour the mixture into one piecrust, and sprinkle with parsley. Cut the pastry from the second crust into 1-inch-wide strips. Place diagonally over the filling.

Place the pie on a baking sheet, and bake 12 to 15 minutes or until the top crust is brown. Cover loosely with aluminum foil, and bake an additional 5 minutes until the pie is cooked through.

Turkey Divan Casserole

YIELD: 6 TO 8 SERVINGS

2 cups broccoli florets, blanched

4 cups cooked turkey, shredded

2 10¾-ounce cans low-sodium cream of chicken soup

1 cup mayonnaise

1 teaspoon curry powder

½ cup breadcrumbs

1 cup shredded cheddar cheese

❖ Preheat the oven to 400°F.

Lightly grease a 9 x 13–inch baking dish.

Place the broccoli in the prepared baking dish. Cover with the turkey. Combine the soup, mayonnaise, and curry powder in a medium bowl, and spoon over the turkey. Sprinkle with the breadcrumbs, and top with the cheese. Bake 30 minutes.

Serve over or alongside rice.

Chicken Enchiladas with Green Sauce

This recipe involves quite a bit of effort, but homemade enchiladas can't be beat for flavor.

⫻

YIELD: 8 SERVINGS

1 4- to 5-pound fresh whole chicken

Salt and pepper, to taste

Onion powder, to taste

Garlic powder, to taste

Cumin, to taste

1-pound block Monterey Jack cheese, grated

1 bunch cilantro, coarsely chopped

1 bunch green onions, finely sliced

1 large white onion, finely chopped

1 16-ounce can black beans, drained and rinsed

4 to 5 Anaheim chilies, roasted, peeled, and chopped

2 16-ounce cans green enchilada sauce

1 8-ounce can black olives, drained

16 medium-size flour tortillas

❖ Place the chicken in a large stockpot. Cover with water, and add salt, pepper, onion powder, garlic powder, and cumin. Bring to a boil, then reduce the heat and simmer until the chicken begins to fall off the bones, about 1 hour.

Remove the chicken from the stockpot, and shred it, discarding fat, skin, and bones. Place the chicken in a large bowl, and add half of the cheese, the cilantro, the green onions, the white onion, and the chilies; mix well. Add enough green enchilada sauce to moisten.

Preheat the oven to 375°F. Lightly grease a 9 x 13–inch baking dish.

Pour a small amount of sauce onto a round plate. Dip a tortilla in the sauce. Put 2 to 3 tablespoons of chicken mixture on the tortilla, roll it up, and place it in the baking dish. Repeat with the remaining tortillas. Cover with the remaining green enchilada sauce. Sprinkle with the remaining cheese, and top with the black olives.

Bake about 15 minutes or until the cheese has melted and the sauce is bubbling.

Chili Con Carne

This recipe helps utilize all those surplus frozen or canned tomatoes from summer. The recipe can be easily halved.

—————————— ¶¶¶ ——————————

YIELD: 10 SERVINGS

2 pounds ground beef

1 cup chopped onion

1 cup chopped bell pepper

1½ cups water

6 teaspoons chili powder

½ teaspoon black pepper

½ teaspoon Tabasco

3 cloves garlic, minced

7 cups heirloom paste tomatoes, such as Opalka, chopped, with juice

2 10¾-ounce cans tomato soup

2 6-ounce cans tomato paste

2 4-ounce cans diced green chilies, drained

1 15-ounce can red kidney beans, drained and rinsed

1 15-ounce can black beans, drained and rinsed

❖ Brown the ground beef and onion in a large cast-iron pot or dutch oven. Add all remaining ingredients except the beans.

Bring mixture to a boil, cover, and simmer for 1 hour, stirring often. Stir in the beans, and simmer for 30 minutes.

Serve with sour cream, grated cheese, and minced onion.

Pot Roasted Creamy Chicken

This old-fashioned, hearty chicken dish is perfect for Sunday dinner when served with roasted carrots, potatoes, and the gravy covering everything. A fresh chicken, harvested straight from your pasture, will provide exceptional flavor and authenticity.

—————————— ¶¶¶ ——————————

YIELD: 4 TO 6 SERVINGS

1 fresh whole chicken, cut into 8 pieces, skin on

Salt and paprika, to taste

¼ cup butter

1 tablespoon vegetable oil

2¼ cups chicken broth

¼ cup sherry

Juice of 1 lemon

1 teaspoon Worcestershire sauce

3½ tablespoons unbleached all-purpose flour

1½ cups heavy cream

❖ Wash and dry the chicken pieces. Sprinkle the meat with the salt and paprika.

Combine the butter and oil in a dutch oven, and brown the chicken on all sides. Add the chicken broth. Cover and simmer for about 45 minutes.

Combine the sherry, lemon juice, and Worcestershire sauce in a small bowl. Whisk in the flour until well mixed. Remove the chicken from the pot, and stir in the flour mixture. Cook 5 minutes, then add the cream, whisking until well blended.

Heat slowly until the sauce thickens. Return the chicken to the pot, and heat an additional 5 minutes.

Curried Flank Steak

YIELD: 6 TO 8 SERVINGS

1½ cups white rice

1 tablespoon extra-virgin olive oil

1½ pounds flank steak, cut into ½-inch strips

2 large heirloom onions, such as White Portugal or Ailsa
   Craig exhibition, cut in ¼-inch slices

¼ cup mild or hot curry paste

1 14-ounce can diced tomatoes

½ cup water

❖ Cook the rice according to the package directions, set aside, and keep warm.

Heat the olive oil in a large nonstick skillet over medium-high heat. Add the flank steak slices, and sauté for 2 minutes. Remove the steak from the skillet, and set aside.

Drain off all but 1 tablespoon of the liquid in the skillet. Add the onion slices to the skillet, and cook 5 to 7 minutes, stirring occasionally. Add the curry paste, and cook for 1 minute. Add the tomatoes, the reserved beef, and the water. Bring to a boil, reduce the heat to medium, and simmer for 3 minutes, stirring often.

Serve over the hot rice.

Roasted Citrus Garlic Chicken

With all the heavy starchy food associated with winter, this citrusy chicken is a nice departure.

❙❙❙

YIELD: 4 TO 6 SERVINGS

1 5- to 6-pound fresh whole heritage chicken

Salt and freshly ground black pepper, to taste

1 orange, quartered

1 lemon, quartered

1 bulb heirloom garlic, such as German Red, halved cross-
   wise, plus 3 cloves garlic, chopped

2 14-ounce cans chicken broth

¼ cup thawed frozen orange juice concentrate

2 tablespoons olive oil

1 tablespoon chopped fresh oregano or sage leaves

❖ Place the oven rack in the center position. Preheat the oven to 400°F.

Remove the neck and giblets from the chicken, then wash and pat the chicken dry. Sprinkle the inside of the chicken with salt and pepper. Stuff the cavity with the orange and lemon quarters. Add the halved bulb of garlic. Tie the chicken legs together with kitchen string to hold its shape.

Sprinkle salt and pepper on the outside of the chicken.

Place the chicken breast side up on a rack in a large roasting pan, and bake 1 hour, basting occasionally. Add some chicken broth to the pan if necessary, to prevent burning.

Whisk the orange juice, olive oil, oregano, and chopped garlic in a medium bowl. Brush on the chicken after it has baked 1 hour. Continue roasting, basting occasionally with the juice mixture and adding broth to the pan, about 45 minutes. Transfer to a platter, and tent with foil while making the sauce.

Place the pan over medium-low heat. Whisk in the remaining broth and simmer, stirring often until it's reduced to 1 cup, about 3 minutes. Strain into a 2-cup glass measuring cup, and spoon the fat from the top of the sauce.

Serve the chicken with the sauce.

HEIRLOOM: HERITAGE CHICKEN

Heritage breeds of chicken such as Plymouth Rock and Dark Cornish are rare and somewhat hard to find. The Plymouth Rock was the first breed to be placed in the American Poultry Association's *American Standard of Perfection* as a purebred in 1873. The Dark Cornish has served as a foundation breed for many modern chicken breeds and was admitted into the *Standard* in 1893. Raised naturally outdoors, heritage chickens are older at slaughter—fifteen weeks, rather than the five weeks in industrial conditions—which com-bined with their pure genetics gives them a flavor different from anything you'll find in the meat department at the grocery.

Rather than the pale pink of a standard chicken, the flesh of her-itage chicken is a beautiful golden yellow because of all of the carotene it consumes in grass. Its meat is darker, denser, richer, and moister than standard chicken meat. A heritage chicken costs more, but the flavor is so superior that it's worth the money. Because heritage chicken differs from supermarket chicken, ask the supplier for the best method of cooking. In general, heritage chicken should be cooked more slowly at a lower temperature.

English Roast Root Vegetables

The lard or shortening gives the vegetables in this recipe a wonderful crispness you just can't achieve with oil.

YIELD: 4 SERVINGS

4 medium heirloom russet potatoes, such as Russet Burbank

3 medium heirloom parsnips, such as The Student

1 cup lard or shortening

Salt and ground black pepper, to taste

❖ Preheat the oven to 425°F.

Peel and quarter the potatoes. Peel and cut the parsnips into equal-size pieces. Parboil the potatoes and parsnips in salted water for about two minutes, then drain well.

Melt the lard or shortening in a large roasting pan in the oven. Add the potatoes and parsnips, being careful not to splash the oil. Roast for 40 to 50 minutes, turning every 10 minutes until browned and crisp on all sides. Drain on paper towels, and season to taste.

Let stand 1 or 2 minutes before serving.

Spicy Pickled Carrots

This pickled mixture is great as an addition to any Mexican meal or to keep in the refrigerator and spoon over chips to serve with salsa. Use a variety of heirloom carrots in this recipe for a multicolored presentation. Long Orange Improved dates back to the 1600s and has a deep orange red root. Early Scarlet Horn was grown before 1610 and is the oldest cultivated carrot still available; it is a short orange stump-rooted variety. The nineteenth-century (1884) Oxheart is a heart-shaped deep orange root with a yellow core. Belgium White dates to 1863 and has a pure white root absent of carotene and a mild flavor. And Red Surrey has a long, tapering orange root with a distinct yellow core.

YIELD: 4 TO 6 SERVINGS

4 heirloom carrots, peeled

2 small onions

12 cloves garlic

1 to 2 jalapeños

1½ cups white vinegar

½ cup white wine

½ cup water

2 bay leaves

1 teaspoon coriander seeds

1 teaspoon cumin seeds

1 teaspoon fennel seeds

10 cilantro stems

1 teaspoon sugar

1 teaspoon salt

Freshly ground pepper, to taste

❖ Slice the carrots and the onions into ¼-inch slices. Peel the garlic and leave whole. Slice the jalapeños into rounds (include the seeds for a spicier mix, or remove seeds, if desired).

Place all the vegetables into a small saucepan and cover with the vinegar, wine, and water. Add the spices, sugar, salt, and pepper. Bring to a boil and simmer 25 minutes or until the carrots are tender. Remove from the heat and chill.

Parsnip Puree

You can serve this with pot roast or even with a hearty fish such as salmon—it creates an interesting flavor combination with the sweet apple and aromatic parsnip.

YIELD: 4 TO 6 SERVINGS

5 medium-size heirloom parsnips, such as The Student

1 medium-size sweet apple

1 medium-size heirloom potato, such as Bintje

3 tablespoons butter

¼ cup heavy cream

Salt and pepper, to taste

❖ Peel and dice the parsnips and apple into medium-size pieces. Dice the potato into small pieces. Place the parsnips, apple, and potato in cold water in a deep saucepan. Bring the water to a boil, reduce the heat, and cook on medium until the potato is tender. Drain well.

Place the mixture in a food processor, and blend for about 2 minutes. Add the butter, cream, salt, and pepper, then pulse for another minute or until the cream and butter are mixed through.

Keep warm until ready to serve.

Cider-Glazed Squash

This side dish is the perfect accompaniment to roasted pork and apple chutney.

YIELD: 4 SERVINGS

2 acorn squash

Salt and pepper, to taste

1 tablespoon olive oil

2 cups cider or unfiltered apple juice

2 tablespoons sugar

4 tablespoons butter

Freshly ground pepper, to taste

❖ Preheat the oven to 400°F.

Lightly grease an 8 x 8–inch baking dish.

Halve the squash, and remove the pith and seeds. Brush with the olive oil. Season the squash with salt and pepper, and place cut side down in a baking dish. Bake for 40 minutes.

While the squash cooks, reduce the cider in a saucepan over medium heat. When the cider has reduced to nearly ½ cup, taste and add sugar if needed. Stir in the butter.

Remove the squash after 40 minutes, and flip the halves so cut side is now up. Brush the cut areas with the cider mixture, and pour the rest evenly over the squash. Bake for an additional 20 minutes or until fork tender.

CIDER-GLAZED SQUASH

GARLIC HERB POTATOES

Garlic Herb Potatoes

Use any variety—Anna Cheeka's Ozette, Russian Banana, Lady Finger, or Cow Horn—of creamy, rich, heirloom fingerling potatoes for this dish.

YIELD: 4 SERVINGS

2 to 3 pounds heirloom fingerling potatoes, scrubbed

4 to 6 tablespoons butter

2 to 4 cloves fresh garlic, finely chopped

½ teaspoon sea salt

HERB COMBINATIONS

2 teaspoons dried or 4 teaspoons fresh thyme, chopped; and
 2 teaspoons dried or 4 teaspoons fresh basil, chopped

or

2 teaspoons dried or fresh rosemary, finely chopped; and 2
 teaspoons dried summer savory, or 4 teaspoons fresh
 savory, chopped

❖ Leaving the skin intact, scrub and slice the potatoes into ¼-inch slices. Place the potatoes in a medium saucepan, and cover with water. Boil the potatoes until tender, approximately 15 minutes, and drain well.

Return the potatoes to the pan. Add the butter, garlic, and salt and one of the herb combinations. Stir until all the butter is melted and the herbs cover the potatoes well.

Serve warm as a side for dinner or as breakfast potatoes.

HEIRLOOM:
ANNA CHEEKA'S OZETTE FINGERLING POTATO

This historic fingerling potato was introduced to North America in the 1700s by Spanish explorers who traded with the Makah tribe of the northwest coast. In the late 1980s, the rare seed was obtained from Anna Cheeka, a Makah Indian at Neah Bay, by David Ronniger, who made it available through Ronniger's Potato Farm. The Ozette (named for the famed Makah village) has pale gold skin and creamy yellow flesh. It grows 2 to 8 inches long and is one of the tastiest of all fingerlings, with a slightly earthy, nutty flavor. The flavor holds up well when the potato is lightly steamed or sautéed.

Homemade Sauerkraut

This recipe is time-consuming (an approximately 6-week process) but worth the effort for the homemade taste. Just be ready with a crock large enough to hold it all.

YIELD: 10 TO 12 SERVINGS

2 pounds heirloom green cabbage, such as Early Jersey Wakefield or Cour di Bue, grated or thinly sliced

1 onion, thinly sliced

5 cloves

10 to 15 black peppercorns

1 teaspoon dill seeds

1 heaping tablespoon sea salt

❖ Grate the cabbage with a cabbage cutter or slice thinly with a large knife. Reserve a few outer leaves of cabbage, and place these on the bottom of a 3- to 4-gallon stoneware crock. Begin layering cabbage to about a 1-inch depth. Add a few slices of onion, a clove, 2 to 3 peppercorns, a sprinkling of dill seeds, and sea salt on top of the cabbage. Add another 1-inch layer of cabbage, and repeat with spices and salt until the cabbage is gone and the crock is nearly full. The cabbage should be soaking in its own juices.

Place a clean cloth on top of the cabbage, place a wooden board or plate on top, and press down so the cabbage juice covers the cabbage by at least 1 inch. Weigh down the board so it remains tightly on the cabbage, place another clean cloth on top, and secure with a rubber band around the crock.

Place the crock in a warm room to start the fermentation process. Make sure the liquid is always covering the cabbage. Move the crock to a cooler spot after a week, and allow the cabbage to ferment for about 6 weeks.

Pack and process the sauerkraut in quart jars using the water-bath method, following the USDA's standards for canning (visit http://www.usda.gov). You can also freeze the sauerkraut in containers.

Sweet Potato Soufflé

This decadent side dish pairs well with fried chicken or ham.

YIELD: 5 SERVINGS

5 medium-size heirloom sweet potatoes, such as Nancy Hall
   or Porto Rico Bush
3 cloves garlic
2 small shallots
2 tablespoons butter
5 large farmstead eggs
½ cup heavy cream, divided
1 tablespoon sea salt
1 teaspoon black pepper
Pinch of nutmeg
Pinch of cayenne pepper

❖ Preheat the oven to 400°F.

Generously butter either one large or five individual ramekins and set aside.

Bake the sweet potatoes 1 hour or until easily pierced with a knife. In the meantime, mince the garlic and the shallots, and place in a medium saucepot. Sauté the garlic and shallots in the butter with a pinch of salt. Remove from the heat.

Separate the eggs, making sure the egg whites are placed in a very clean stainless steel bowl. Cut the cooked sweet potatoes in half and remove the flesh, and add it to the garlic and shallots in the saucepan, along with half the cream.

Return the pan to the stove over low heat. Using a pastry cutter or fork, mash the potatoes, and mix well with the garlic and shallots. Add the salt, pepper, nutmeg, and cayenne. Taste to ensure the mixture is highly seasoned. Remove the saucepan from the heat.

In a large bowl, beat the egg yolks with the remaining cream and a large spoonful of the sweet potatoes to warm the yolks. Slowly add the sweet potatoes to the yolk mixture, being careful not to cook the yolks.

Beat the egg whites in a medium bowl with an electric mixer until stiff peaks have formed, but do not over-whip the whites. Carefully fold the egg whites one-third at a time into the yolk mixture, and mix well.

Fill the ramekins two-thirds full and place in the oven. You will need to watch the soufflés, but do not open the oven for at least 20 minutes for small molds. A larger mold may take up to 1 hour. The soufflés should be puffed, golden, and pulling slightly away from the edges of the container.

Roast Squash with Curry and Walnuts

YIELD: 4 SERVINGS

2 medium heirloom winter squash, such as Butternut

4 tablespoons olive oil

2 teaspoons sea salt

1 tablespoon coarsely ground pepper

1 cup walnuts

½ cup honey

1 tablespoon curry powder

HEIRLOOM: BUTTERNUT SQUASH

Introduced in 1944, the Butternut comes from old heirloom stock and is considered a fall staple for preparing in sautés and baked goods. The Butternut squash is a medium-size, buff-colored, bottle-shaped fruit that weighs about 5 pounds. Its rind is thin enough to peel off with a vegetable peeler, and its dry, fine-textured orange flesh is an excellent source of beta carotene and vitamin A. The flavor is sweet, moist, and pleasantly nutty (more so than that of the Buttercup).

❖ Preheat the oven to 400°F.

Split the squash, and remove the seeds. Drizzle each half with 1 tablespoon olive oil, ½ tablespoon sea salt, and ¼ teaspoon black pepper.

Lay the squash cut side down on baking sheets, and bake for 45 minutes to 1 hour or until easily pierced with a knife. Remove the squash from the oven, and flip so the cut side is facing upward.

Divide the walnuts, honey, and curry powder evenly among the squash halves, and return to oven for an additional 10 minutes.

Sweet Potato Casserole

This dish makes a great addition to a holiday entrée but is sweet enough for dessert.

YIELD: 8 SERVINGS

5 cups (about 5 to 6 medium-size potatoes) mashed heirloom sweet potatoes, such as Nancy Hall or Southern Queen

1 cup sugar

⅓ cup milk

1½ tablespoons melted butter

3 large farmstead eggs

2 teaspoons pure vanilla extract

1 cup shredded coconut

1 cup packed dark brown sugar

1 cup chopped pecans

¼ cup melted butter

❖ Preheat the oven to 300°F.

Lightly grease a 9 × 13–inch baking dish.

Combine the sweet potatoes, sugar, milk, 1½ tablespoons butter, eggs, and vanilla in a large bowl. Beat all ingredients until smooth. Pour into the prepared baking dish, and bake 15 minutes.

Combine the coconut, brown sugar, and pecans in a medium bowl and mix well. Add the ¼ cup melted butter, and mix until crumbly. Add more butter if needed. Spread over the potatoes, and bake about 20 minutes or until the topping browns slightly.

Winter Squash Casserole

YIELD: 12 SERVINGS

6 cups cooked, mashed heirloom winter squash, such as
    Buttercup, Butternut, or Golden Hubbard

6 large farmstead eggs, beaten

½ teaspoon salt

½ cup melted butter or margarine

1 cup sugar*

1 cup dark brown sugar

½ cup butter or margarine

¼ cup unbleached all-purpose flour

½ cup slivered almonds

❖ Preheat the oven to 350°F.

Combine the squash, eggs, salt, melted butter, and 1 cup sugar in a large bowl, and mix well. Place in an ungreased 9 x 13–inch baking dish.

Combine the brown sugar, ½ cup butter, flour, and almonds in a medium bowl. Mix until crumbly, and spoon on top of the squash casserole. Bake uncovered 45 minutes or until a knife comes out clean when inserted in the center.

*For less sweetness, do not add the 1 cup sugar, and use only the brown sugar that is part of the topping.

HEIRLOOM:
BUTTERCUP SQUASH

Buttercup is a turban-shaped winter squash and is considered the tastiest of the turban squashes. It was developed by the North Dakota Agricultural Experiment Station by accident—a cross between Quality and Essex Hybrid—in the 1920s. Fruits of the Buttercup are small and flattened with a button on the blossom end. The skin is dark green and thick, with dry, sweet, and golden-colored flesh.

Fried Parsnips with Bacon

YIELD: 8 SERVINGS

1 pound (about 8 medium) heirloom parsnips, such as The
   Student

4 to 5 thick slices of bacon

1 cup unbleached all-purpose flour

Salt and black pepper, to taste

4 to 6 tablespoons butter

2 tablespoons chopped fresh parsley

❖ Remove the top and root ends from the parsnips and peel them. Cut them in half the short direction, then slice each half lengthwise to form ¼-inch-thick slices. Cook in boiling salted water in a medium saucepan until tender.

Meanwhile, fry the bacon until crisp. Remove the bacon from the fat, and drain on paper towels, then crumble and set aside. Strain the fat through a mesh strainer, then set aside.

Combine the flour, salt, and pepper in a shallow dish. Dredge each parsnip slice in flour.

In a large, heavy-bottomed frying pan, combine the bacon fat and the butter, and heat on medium-high until hot, but not smoking. Add the floured parsnip slices, and fry until golden; then turn parsnips and brown the other side.

Serve topped with crumbled bacon, and garnish with chopped fresh parsley.

HEIRLOOM: THE STUDENT PARSNIP

The parsnip originated in Europe, with the earliest known cultivation dating to the Roman period. English settlers brought the parsnip to the American colonies in the 1600s, and it remained a popular vegetable in the United States through the nineteenth century.

The English have always held this root vegetable in high regard. The variety known as The Student was developed in 1859 at the Royal Agriculture College in Cirencester, England, from a wild parsnip growing in a field in the Cotswolds. Being closely related to the earliest strains of parsnips, The Student came to be considered by some as the best variety in cultivation. It has become a favorite with kitchen gardeners because of its consistent yield and its ability to keep well. The Student's thick, tapering roots grow to about 15 inches, and its sweet, mild flavor makes it ideal for baking and for soups.

Figgy Pudding

You may know figgy pudding from the second verse of the time-honored Christmas carol "We Wish You a Merry Christmas." Now you can make your own figgy pudding to have on hand for those persistent Christmas carolers.

YIELD: 6 TO 8 SERVINGS

½ cup softened butter

2 large farmstead eggs

1 cup unsulfured molasses

2 cups finely chopped dried figs

½ teaspoon grated orange zest

1 cup buttermilk

½ cup toasted and chopped walnuts

2½ cups unbleached all-purpose flour

2 teaspoons baking powder

½ teaspoon baking soda

1 teaspoon kosher salt

1 teaspoon pumpkin spice

❖ Preheat the oven to 325°F. Grease and flour an 8 x 4-inch soufflé dish, and set aside.

Cream the butter in a large bowl until fluffy. Add the eggs and molasses, and blend well. Add the figs, orange zest, buttermilk, and walnuts, and blend 1 minute. Add the remaining ingredients, and mix until blended.

Spoon the batter into the prepared soufflé dish. Bake 1 hour or until toothpick inserted off center comes out clean.

Spoon onto plates, and serve warm with cinnamon-flavored whipped cream or ice cream.

FIGS

The ancient history of the fig centers around the Mediterranean region with biblical passages noting the tree, leaves, and fruit. Figs are most commonly cultivated in temperate climates such as the Middle East; the Mediterranean; India; and parts of the United States, including California, Florida, Texas, and Washington. They were first introduced into the New World by Spanish and Portuguese missionaries, the first plantings occurring in Mexico in 1560.

There are many varieties of figs. The common fig is teardrop in

shape, measures about 1 to 4 inches long, and has thin purple-brown skin and pinkish flesh. Fresh figs are perishable, so the majority of figs are consumed in the dried state.

In warm, humid climates, figs are generally eaten fresh and raw, when they are sweeter than honey, and served with cream and sugar. The fruits may be stewed or cooked in various ways, as in pies, puddings, cakes, breads, and other bakery products, or added to ice cream. Backyard growers preserve the whole fruits in sugar syrup or prepare them as jam, marmalade, or paste. Fig paste makes up the well-known Fig Newton cookies. Commercially, the fruits are also candied whole.

Easy Lemon Tarts

⦚▮⦚

YIELD: 10 TO 12 SERVINGS

1 double-crust pie dough (any type of unbaked, raw piecrust
 dough)

2 large farmstead eggs

1 14-ounce can sweetened condensed milk

⅔ cup freshly squeezed Meyer lemon juice, strained to
 remove seeds and pulp

1 tablespoon finely grated lemon zest

Whipped cream (optional)

Additional lemon zest (optional)

❖ Preheat the oven to 450°F.

Roll out the piecrust. Use a 4-inch round cookie cutter (or a 4-inch round lid and paring knife) to cut out 10 to 12 circles. Invert one 12-muffin or two 6-muffin pans, and place circles of dough over the bottoms of the muffin cups, crimping each to form a shell. Bake for 10 to 12 minutes or until the tart shells start to brown lightly. Remove from the oven. When cool enough to handle, lift the tart shells off the muffin pan, and finish cooling right side up on a wire rack.

Beat the eggs until slightly thickened. Stir in the sweetened condensed milk, lemon juice, and zest. Spoon into the tart shells, and refrigerate until firm, about 2 hours.

Serve with whipped cream or garnish with additional lemon zest, if desired.

Holiday Persimmon Pudding

⦚▮⦚

YIELD: 6 TO 8 SERVINGS

1 cup seedless white or black raisins

1 cup chopped roasted walnuts

½ cup sugar

½ cup packed light brown sugar

2 cups unbleached all-purpose flour

1 tablespoon pumpkin spice

½ teaspoon kosher salt

1½ teaspoons baking soda

1 teaspoon baking powder

2 large farmstead eggs, beaten

1 cup whole milk

½ cup melted butter or margarine

1 cup chopped ripe persimmons

❖ Preheat the oven to 325°F. Grease and flour a 9 X 9–inch baking pan.

Place raisins, walnuts, and sugars in a medium-size bowl. Sift together the flour, pumpkin spice, salt, and baking soda into the bowl, and mix well. Add the eggs, milk, and melted butter, and mix well. Fold in the persimmons.

Spoon the batter into the prepared pan. Bake for 1 hour or until wooden skewer inserted into middle of pan comes out clean or with only a few crumbs. Do not overbake.

Serve warm with homemade lemon curd (recipe on page 219).

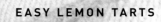

EASY LEMON TARTS

HOME-CANNED LEMON CURD

Home-Canned Lemon Curd

Lemon curd is a thick lemon preserve that works as a pie filling, toast topper, cookie dip, ice cream sauce . . . there are myriad possibilities.

YIELD: 3 TO 4 HALF-PINT JARS

2¼ cups sugar

½ cup finely grated Meyer lemon peel

1 cup freshly squeezed Meyer lemon juice (remove seeds)

¾ cup chilled butter, cut into 1-inch pieces

7 large farmstead egg yolks

4 large farmstead eggs

❖ Wash and sterilize half-pint jars, lids, and rings. Fill water bath canner with enough water to cover filled jars by 2 inches, and start heating water.*

Combine the sugar and lemon peel and set aside.

Heat the water in the bottom pan of a double boiler until it boils gently. (The water should not boil vigorously or touch the bottom of the top double-boiler pan.)

Meanwhile, in the top of the double boiler (do not place it over the bottom pan yet), whisk together the 7 egg yolks and 4 eggs. Slowly whisk in the sugar and zest, blending until smooth. Add the lemon juice and then the butter pieces to the mixture.

Place the top of the double boiler over gently boiling water in the bottom pan. Cook, stirring gently, until the mixture reaches a temperature of 170°F on a food thermometer.

Remove the double boiler from the heat, and place on a protected surface, such as a towel or a wooden board. Continue to stir gently until curd thickens (about 5 minutes). Strain the curd through a mesh strainer into a glass or a stainless steel bowl. Discard collected zest.

Pour the hot curd into hot half-pint jars, leaving ½-inch headspace. Wipe the rims of the jars with a damp paper towel, and fasten lids and rings. Place the jars in a 180°F water bath (see note below), and increase heat. When the water boils over the tops of the jars, process for 15 minutes. Let cool, undisturbed, for 12 to 24 hours, then check seals.

* Use a thermometer to monitor water temperature. The water should be 180°F when you add the filled jars, so it will take about 25 to 30 minutes to reach boiling after you add the jars. The extra heating time is necessary for safely processing this particular recipe. Begin processing time when the water comes to a full boil over the tops of the jars.

HEIRLOOM: MEYER LEMON

The Meyer lemon tree originated in China and was introduced to the United States in 1908 by Frank Meyer, an employee of the United States Department of Agriculture, who brought back a sample of the plant after traveling in China. The Meyer lemon was elevated to gourmet food status in the United States after being rediscovered by chefs such as Alice Waters during the California cuisine revolution of the 1970s.

The Meyer lemon is believed to be a cross between a true lemon and a mandarin orange. Its leaves are dark green and shiny, and the flowers are white with a purple base. The small round fruit is yellow with an orange tint when ripe. Its skin is thin and soft, fragrant and edible, making it a favorite of chefs and gourmets. Meyer lemons are slightly sweeter and less acidic than are the commercial varieties (such as Eureka and Lisbon).

Port Poached Pears

YIELD: 3 SERVINGS

3 Comice pears

4 to 5 cups port

½ cup sugar

2 cloves

1 star anise

2 cinnamon sticks

6 allspice berries

2 juniper berries

COMICE PEAR

The Comice pear, known properly as Doyenné du Comice, is a French variety first propagated near Angers in the mid-1800s. Comice is the sweetest and juiciest of all pear varieties, and its flesh is very soft with a creamy texture. Most pear lovers consider Comice the gold standard for the fruit.

The Comice grows in all sizes, but its shape is distinguishable from other varieties—a rotund body with a very short, well-defined neck. It is most often green in color and sometimes has a red blush sweeping across small to large areas of its skin. The succulent Comice can grow to be very large, and the jumbo-size beauties are often the ones that appear in holiday gift boxes.

You can find Comice pears, grown in Oregon and Washington, in many grocery store produce departments for several months of the year, usually September through March.

❖ Using a vegetable peeler or paring knife, gently peel the pears.

In a saucepan, combine the port, sugar, and spices. Add the pears plus enough water to cover. Heat this mixture until it is barely at a simmer, and cook the pears for about 1 hour or until they are easily pierced with a knife.

Remove the pears from the poaching liquid; and adjust the heat to high to boil and reduce the liquid, about 20 to 25 minutes. Once the liquid has reduced to about 1 cup, remove from the heat. The port should be syrupy. Taste and adjust with sugar or lemon juice if necessary.

Serve the pears with ice cream or whipped cream, and drizzle with the syrup.

PORT POACHED PEARS

Appendix A: Heirloom Seed Sources and Heritage Meat Suppliers

HEIRLOOM SEED SOURCES

Abundant Life Seeds
PO Box 157
Saginaw, OR 97472-0157
541-767-9606
http://www.abundantlifeseeds.com

Appalachian Heirloom Seed
Conservancy
PO Box 519
Richmond, KY 40476
KentuckySeeds@hotmail.com

Artistic Gardens
PO Box 75
St. Johnsbury Center, VT 05863-0075
802-748-1446
http://www.artisticgardens.com

Baker Creek Heirloom Seed
Company
2278 Baker Creek Road
Mansfield, MO 65704
417-924-8917
http://www.rareseeds.com

Bountiful Gardens
18001 Shafer Ranch Road
Willits, CA 95490
707-459 6410
http://www.bountifulgardens.org

D.V. Burrell Seed Growers
Company
PO Box 150
Rocky Ford, CO 81067
719-254-3318
http://www.burrellseeds.com

Comstock, Ferre & Co.
263 Main Street
Wethersfield, CT 06109

800-733-3773
http://www.comstockferre.com

The Cook's Garden
PO Box 535
Londonderry, VT 05148
800-457-9703
http://www.cooksgarden.com

Fedco Seeds and Trees
PO Box 520
Waterville, ME 04903
207-873-7333
http://www.fedcoseeds.com

Filaree Farm
182 Conconully Highway
Okanogan, WA 98840
509-422 6940
http://www.filareefarm.com

Garden Medicinals and Culinaries
PO Box 320
Earlysville, VA 22936
434-964-9113
http://www.gardenmedicinals.com

The Gourmet Gardener
12287 117th Drive
Live Oak, FL 32060
386-362-9089
http://www.gourmetgardener.com

Harris Seeds
355 Paul Road
PO Box 24966
Rochester, NY 14624-0966
800-514-4441
http://www.harrisseeds.com

Heirloom Seeds
PO Box 245
West Elizabeth, PA 15088-0245
412-384-0852
http://www.heirloomseeds.com

Irish Eyes–Garden City Seeds
PO Box 307
Thorp, WA 98946
509-964-7000
http://www.gardencityseeds.net

Johnny's Selected Seeds
955 Benton Avenue
Winslow, ME 04901
877-564-6697
http://www.johnnyseeds.com

Jordan Seeds
6400 Upper Afton Road
Woodbury, MN 55125
651-738-3422
http://www.jordanseeds.com

Kitazawa Seed Company
PO Box 13220
Oakland, CA 94661-3220
510-595-1188
http://www.kitazawaseed.com

Milk Ranch Specialty Potatoes
20094 Highway 149
Powderhorn, CO 81243
970-641-5634
http://www.milkranch.com

Native Seeds/SEARCH
526 N. 4th Avenue
Tucson, AZ 85705-8450
866-622-5561
http://www.nativeseeds.org

Nichols Garden Nursery
1190 Old Salem Road NE
Albany, OR 97321-4580
800-422-3985
http://www.nicholsgardennursery.com

Old House Gardens
536 Third Street
Ann Arbor, MI 48103-4957

734-995-1486
http://www.oldhousegardens.com

Ornamental Edibles
5723 Trowbridge Way
San Jose, CA 95138
408-528-7333
http://www.ornamentaledibles.com

Peaceful Valley Farm & Garden
Supply
PO Box 2209
Grass Valley, CA 95945
888-784-1722
http://www.groworganic.com

The Pepper Gal
PO Box 23006
Ft. Lauderdale, FL 33307
954-537-5540
http://www.peppergal.com

Pinetree Garden Seeds
PO Box 300
New Gloucester, ME 04260
207-926-3400
http://www.superseeds.com

Redwood City Seed Company
PO Box 361
Redwood City, CA 94064
650-325-7333
http://www.ecoseeds.com

Renee's Garden
6116 Highway 9
Felton, CA 95018
888-880-7228
http://www.reneesgarden.com

R. H. Shumway's
334 W. Stroud Street
Randolph, WI 53956-1274
800-342-9461
http://www.rhshumway.com

Ronniger's Potato Farm
20094 N State Highway 149
Powderhorn, CO 81243
877-204-8704
http://www.ronnigers.com

Sand Hill Preservation Center
1878 230th Street
Calamus, IA 52729
563-246-2299
http://www.sandhillpreservation.com

Seeds of Change
PO Box 15700
Santa Fe, NM 87506-5700
888-762-7333
http://www.seedsofchange.com

Seed Savers Exchange
3094 North Winn Road
Decorah, IA 52101
563-382-5990
http://www.seedsavers.org

Select Seeds
180 Stickney Hill Road
Union, CT 06076
800-684-0395
http://www.selectseeds.com

Southern Exposure Seed Exchange
PO Box 460
Mineral, VA 23117
540-894-9480
http://www.southernexposure.com

Sustainable Mountain Agriculture
Center
1033 Pilot Knob Cemetery Road
Berea, KY 40403
859-986-3204
http://www.heirlooms.org

Territorial Seed Company
PO Box 158

Cottage Grove, OR 97424-0061
800-626-0866
http://www.territorial-seed.com

Thomas Jefferson Center for
Historic Plants
Monticello, PO Box 316
Charlottesville, VA 22902
434-984-9822
http://www.monticello.org/chp
/index.html

Tomato Growers Supply
Company
PO Box 60015
Fort Myers, FL 33906
888-478-7333
http://www.tomatogrowers.com

Totally Tomatoes
334 West Stroud Street
Randolph, WI 53956-1274
800-345-5977
http://www.totallytomato.com

Trees of Antiquity
20 Wellsona Road
Paso Robles, CA 93446
805-467-9909
http://www.treesofantiquity.com

Vermont Bean Seed Company
334 W. Stroud Street
Randolph, WI 53956-1274
800-349-1071
http://www.vermontbean.com

Willhite Seed, Inc.
PO Box 23
Poolville, TX 76487-0023
800-828-1840
http://www.willhiteseed.com

Wood Prairie Farm
49 Kinney Road

Bridgewater, ME 04735
800-829-9765
http://www.woodprairie.com

HERITAGE MEAT SUPPLIERS

Bailey Cattle Company
3 Ridgewood Lane
Searcy, AR 72143
501-268-8105
http://www.baileycattle.com
Beef, heritage turkey, chickens, and eggs

CloverDale Farms
11375 South 37th Street
Scotts, MI 49088
269-626-0030
tbartathome@aol.com
Belted Galloway grass-fed beef, pork, chicken, and eggs

Creswick Farms
6500 Rollenhagen Road
Ravenna, MI 49451
616-837-9226
http://www.creswickfarms.com
Beef, pork, turkey, chicken, and eggs

Dayspring Farm
217 Darby Hill
Rockingham, VT 05101
802-463-2205
http://www.dayspringfarm.com
Grass-fed dexter and lowline beef

Earth Shine Farm
9580 New Lothrop Road
Durand, MI 48429
989-288-2421
http://www.earthshinefarm.com
Heritage chicken and eggs

Fallow Hollow Deer Farm
Williams Road
Candor, NY 13743
607-659-4635
http://www.fallowhollow.com
Deer, poultry, pork, beef, and rabbit

Flying Pigs Farm
246 Sutherland Road
Shushan, NY 12873
518-854-3844
http://www.flyingpigsfarm.com
Heritage pork

Greenwood Farms
16800 State Route T
Newburg, MO 65550
800-253-6574
http://www.greenwoodfarms.com
Grass-fed heritage pork, lamb, beef, chicken, and eggs

Gryffon's Aerie
8205 James Madison Highway
Gordonsville, VA 22942
540-967-5632
http://www.gryffonsaerie.com
Devon and belted Galloway beef, Tamworth pork, and Cotswold lamb

Heritage Foods USA
PO Box 827
New York, NY 10150
212-980-6603
http://www.heritagefoodsusa.com
Heritage beef, pork, turkey, duck, bison, and fish

Kay's HomeFarm
8707 Kaehler's Mill Road
Cedarburg, WI 53012
262-375-1702
http://www.kaysfarm.com
Grass-fed black Galloway beef

King Bird Farm
9398 W. Creek Rd.
Berkshire, NY 13736
607-657-2860
http://www.kingbirdfarm.com
Certified-organic pork, chicken, turkey, eggs, grass-fed Highland X Angus beef

Local Harvest
220 21st Avenue
Santa Cruz, CA 95062
831-475-8150
http://www.localharvest.org
Database of farms selling heritage meat and heirloom products

Lobel's of New York
1096 Madison Avenue
New York, NY 10028
800-556-2357
http://www.lobels.com
Heritage beef, pork, and lamb

Mary's Free-Range Turkey
6567 N. Tamera Avenue
Fresno, CA 93711
888-666-8244
http://www.marysturkeys.com
Free-range heritage turkey

Morgan & York
1928 Packard
Ann Arbor, MI 48104
734-662-0798
http://www.bigtenmarket.com
Heritage chicken

Naylor Family Farm
5369 Plot Road
Johnson, VT 05656
802-644-6567
Pasture-raised, certified-organic British white beef

Frather Ranch Meat Company
Cne Ferry Plaza, Shop #32
San Francisco, CA 94111
415-391-0420
http://www.prmeatco.com
Tamworth and Berkshire pork, beef,
lamb, and buffalo

Shuttleworth Farm
649 Loop Road
Westfield, VT 05874
802-744-6431
http://www.shuttleworthfarm.com
Grass-fed devon beef, pork, and
lamb

Skate Creek Farm
1496 County Highway 12
East Meredith, NY 13757
607-278-5602
http://www.skatecreekfarm.com
Beef, pork, poultry, lamb, and eggs

Stone & Thistle Farm
1211 Kelso Road
East Meredith, NY 13757
607-278-5773
http://www.stoneandthistlefarm.com
Heritage pork, beef, goat, lamb,
chicken, turkey, and rabbit

Townline Farm Poultry Reserve
14563 Townline Road
Linesville, PA 16424-5953
877-632-9242
http://www.townlinefarm.com
Heritage turkey, geese, chicken, and
eggs

Windswept Farm Katahdin Sheep
3649 E. Sherwood Road
Williamston, MI 48895
517-468-2246
Grass-fed Katahdin lamb

Appendix B: Resources on Heirloom Gardening and Cooking

BOOKS

Coulter, Lynn. *Gardening with Heirloom Seeds: Tried-and-True Flowers, Fruits, and Vegetables for a New Generation.* Chapel Hill: University of North Carolina Press, 2006.

Creasy, Rosalind. *The Edible Heirloom Garden.* North Clarendon, VT: Periplus, 1999.

Ekarius, Carol. *Hobby Farm: Living Your Rural Dream for Pleasure and Profit.* Irvine, CA: BowTie Press, 2005.

Gardner, Jo Ann. *The Heirloom Garden: Selecting and Growing Over 300 Old-Fashioned Ornamentals.* North Adams, MA: Storey Books, 1992.

Goldman, Amy. *Melons for the Passionate Grower.* New York: Artisan, 2002.

Goldman, Amy. *The Compleat Squash.* New York: Artisan, 2004.

Jabs, Carolyn. T*he Heirloom Gardener: Collecting and Growing Old and Rare Varieties of Vegetables and Fruits: All About Heirloom Plants and How Gardeners Can Help Save this Living Legacy.* San Francisco: Sierra Club Books, 1984.

Male, Carolyn J. *100 Heirloom Tomatoes for the American Garden.* New York: Workman Publishing, 1999.

Staub, Jack. *75 Exciting Vegetables for Your Garden.* Layton, UT: Gibbs Smith, 2005.

Stickland, Sue. *Heirloom Vegetables: A Home Gardener's Guide to Finding and Growing Vegetables from the Past.* New York: Fireside (Simon & Schuster), 1998.

Watson, Benjamin. *Taylor's Guide to Heirloom Vegetables: A Complete Guide to the Best Historic and Ethnic Varieties.* Boston, MA: Houghton Mifflin, 1996.

Weaver, William Woys. *100 Vegetables and Where They Came From.* New York: Algonquin Books (Workman Publishing), 2000.

Weaver, William Woys. *Heirloom Vegetable Gardening: A Master Gardener's Guide to Planting, Seed Saving, and Cultural History.* New York: Henry Holt, 1997.

Yepsen, Roger. *A Celebration of Heirloom Vegetables: Growing and Cooking Old-Time Varieties.* New York: Artisan, 1998.

PERIODICALS

The Heirloom Gardener
PO Box 70
Mansfield, MO 65704-0070
417-924-1222
http://www.rareseeds.com

Hobby Farms™, *Hobby Farms Home*™, and *Popular Farming*™ Magazines
P.O. Box 6050
Mission Viejo, CA 92690-6050

(949) 855-8822
Fax (949) 855-3045
http://www.hobbyfarms.com

Index